Paperback ISBN: 978-1-63744-086-5

Hardcover ISBN: 978-1-63744-097-1

Intermediate
Word 365

WORD 365 ESSENTIALS - BOOK 2

M.L. HUMPHREY

CONTENTS

CONTENTS (CONT.)

Introduction

In *Word 365 for Beginners* we covered the basics of Microsoft Word including text, paragraph, and page formatting; numbered lists; bulleted lists; and printing. But there's a lot more you can do in Word and that's what this book is for, to take your use of Word to the next level.

The key topics we're going to cover here are Styles, Page and Section Breaks, Multilevel Lists, Tables, and Track Changes. We'll also revisit headers and footers briefly and cover some minor topics such as inserting symbols, footnotes, and watermarks. It won't be everything you can do in Word, but it will cover a substantial part of it.

This book is written using Word 365 as it exists in January 2023 and written using the desktop version of the program. All screenshots use the Colorful Theme.

Okay, then, let's just dive right in with one of my favorite little tricks to use in Word: Styles. But first, a quick recap of basic terminology so you know what I mean when I say things.

Basic Terminology Recap

These terms were covered in detail in *Word 365 for Beginners*. This is just meant as a refresher.

Tab

When I refer to a tab, I am referring to the menu options at the top of the screen. The tab options that are available by default are File, Home, Insert, Draw, Design, Layout, References, Mailings, Review, View, and Help, but for certain tasks additional tabs will appear.

Click

If I tell you to click on something, that means to move your cursor over to that location and then either right-click or left-click. If I don't say which to do, left-click.

Left-Click / Right-Click

A left-click is generally for selecting something and involves using the left-hand side of your mouse or bottom left-hand corner of your trackpad. A right-click is generally for opening a dropdown menu and involves using the right-hand side of your mouse or bottom right-hand corner of your trackpad.

Left-Click and Drag

Left-click and drag means to left-click and then hold that left-click as you move your mouse.

Dropdown Menu

A dropdown menu is a list of choices that you can view by right-clicking in a specific spot or clicking on an arrow next to or below one of the available choices under the tabs up top. Depending on where you are in the workspace, a dropdown menu may actually drop upward from that spot.

Expansion Arrow

In the bottom right corner of some of the sections under the tabs in the top menu you will see an arrow, which I refer to as an expansion arrow. Clicking on an expansion arrow will usually open a dialogue box or task pane and is often the way to see the largest number of options.

Dialogue Box

A dialogue box is a pop-up box that will open on top of your workspace and will usually include the largest number of choices for that particular setting or task.

Scroll Bar

Scroll bars appear when there are more options than can appear on the screen or when your document is longer than will show on the screen. They can be used to move through the remainder of the choices or document.

Task Pane

A task pane is a set of additional options that will appear to the sides or even below the main workspace. The Navigation pane is by default visible on the left-hand side of the workspace. You can close a task pane by clicking on the X in the top right corner of the pane.

Control Shortcuts

Control shortcuts are shortcuts that let you perform certain tasks in Word. I will write them as Ctrl + and then a character. That means to hold down both the Ctrl key and that character. So Ctrl + C means hold down Ctrl and C, which will let you copy your selection. Even though I will write each shortcut using a capital letter it doesn't have to be the capitalized version to work.

Styles

If you're going to do any formatting in Word, using styles will save you a tremendous amount of time and effort.

For example, the first print books I ever formatted I used Word. And I was able to set up three styles that I could use, one for the chapter names, one for the first paragraph of a chapter or section, and one for all other paragraphs. It was then a very simple matter to apply the "all other paragraphs" format to my entire document and then go through and for each chapter header and each first paragraph in a chapter or section apply the other formats.

That easily let me create a document with consistent formatting throughout.

A style has the font, font size, color, paragraph spacing, paragraph indent, etc. all built in, so you don't have to keep changing those settings. It's much better at ensuring consistency of appearance than trying to format your paragraphs manually. And much easier to apply than the Format Painter option.

Also, you can create shortcuts for your styles so that you don't even have to use your mouse, you can just use your keyboard shortcut to apply each style.

Alright. Let's walk through how to use them now.

Styles are located in the Styles section of the Home tab:

The number of styles that are visible by default will depend on your screen size, but usually it will be a handful or so. There is a downward-pointing arrow on the right-hand side of that listing (see the screenshot above) that you can click on to expand the list of styles. If you do so, it will look something like this:

in Excel. (If not, check out one of those books).

Those are all of the default styles that Word uses. Each one is formatted to show a bit of what that style will look like if applied to your text.

When I'm drafting a document like this one, I usually have my paragraphs use the Normal style and my chapters use the Heading 1 style. I then change the styles when I'm done and ready to format.

The Normal style will be applied to your text by default so you don't have to do anything to use it. But the Heading 1 style does have to be applied.

To apply a style to your text, click onto that paragraph or line of text. (You don't have to select all of the text, just click onto some portion of that paragraph or line of text.) Next, click on the style you want from the Style listing in the Styles section of the Home tab.

The Normal and Heading styles can also be applied using a control shortcut. Ctrl + Shift + N will apply the Normal style. Ctrl + Alt + 1 will apply Heading 1, Ctrl + Alt + 2 will apply Heading 2, and Ctrl + Alt + 3 will apply Heading 3.

If you use the Heading styles, Word will also show any text with those styles applied in your Navigation pane on the left-hand side under the Headings view. Here you can see my chapter names, Introduction, Terminology, Shortcuts, etc. from *Excel Tips and Tricks*, all of which were formatted using the Heading 1 style:

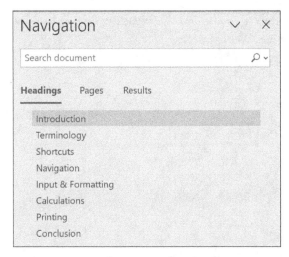

Click on each of those entries to go to that part of your document.

You can also left-click and drag one of those entries in that list to move the entire section to a new location in your document. The text that moves will be all text from that header through to the next text in the document that has that same heading style or a higher-level heading style.

Meaning, that if I have applied the Heading 1 style to all of my chapter titles and I left-click and drag one of my chapter titles to a new location in the list, that will move that entire chapter to the new location. But it will leave all subsequent chapters where they are.

Here, for example, I dragged Conclusion to the top above Introduction, which you can see on the left-hand-side listing. You can also see by looking at the document that all text from the chapter moved, too:

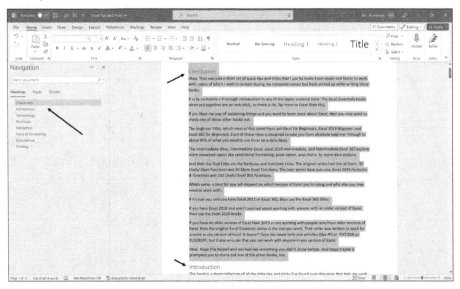

Here is an example where I've applied the Heading 2 style to the chapter sub-sections, Pin a File and Navigate Between Worksheets:

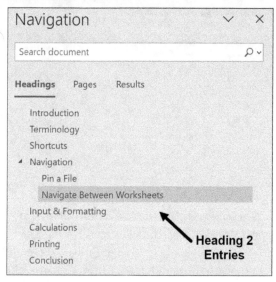

If I click and drag one of the Heading 2 entries, all text between that entry and the next listed heading will move. So if I move Pin a File, all text from there to Navigate Between Worksheets will move. But if I move Navigate Between Worksheets, all text from there to the next chapter, Input & Formatting, will move.

I know that sounds very complex, but if you need to do this, the best way to learn is to try it out and see what happens. I very rarely need to click and drag to move an entire section of my document, but it does sometimes happen. If the idea of doing so using the Headings listing scares you, there's always cut and paste.

Also, when you use a Heading level, like I did here with Heading 2, Word will automatically make the next heading level, in this case, Heading 3, available in the Styles section.

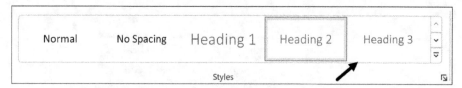

When you use the heading styles in your document, that also allows you to collapse those sections so the text under that heading is hidden, like I've done here for Pin a File:

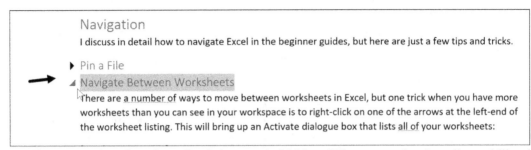

You still have the heading, but all of the text is hidden. When a section is collapsed like that, the black arrow to the left of the heading will be visible. Click on that to expand the section once more.

To collapse a section, you need to hold your mouse over the header to make that blue arrow appear on the left-hand side like I've done above for Navigate Between Worksheets. Click on that arrow to collapse the section and hide the text.

Headings are useful when drafting a large document, but the default Word styles are usually not what I want to use for my final document, so once I'm done I need to create custom styles or apply styles from another document.

Let's walk through how to do that now.

First off, I'm not a fan of messing with the default styles. So I try to leave Normal and the Headings alone. I won't directly modify those if I can avoid it.

Instead, what I do is I take a paragraph and I modify it so that it's formatted the way I want.

(If I have another document that is already formatted properly I will use the Format Painter from the Clipboard section of the Home tab to bring in that formatting for me. Sometimes that also brings in a style name, too, and I don't have to do the rest of these steps to create a new style, I can just apply it where needed. But assuming it doesn't…)

Next, once my paragraph is formatted the way I want, I expand the Styles section and click on the option to Create a Style. That brings up the Create New Style From Formatting dialogue box:

Create New Style from Formatting	?	✕

Name:

Style1

Paragraph style preview:

Style1

OK	Modify…	Cancel

I change the name of the style to something that I'll remember and then click OK. That adds that style as an option in the Styles section of the Home tab:

I can then click on that option to format any other paragraph in my document using that style. (We'll talk in a moment about how to do this quickly.)

If you want there to be a keyboard shortcut for that style, right-click on the style in the Styles section and choose Modify from the dropdown menu. That will open the Modify Style dialogue box. At the bottom of that dialogue box is a dropdown menu that says Format. Click on that to see a list of choices. The one you want is Shortcut Key:

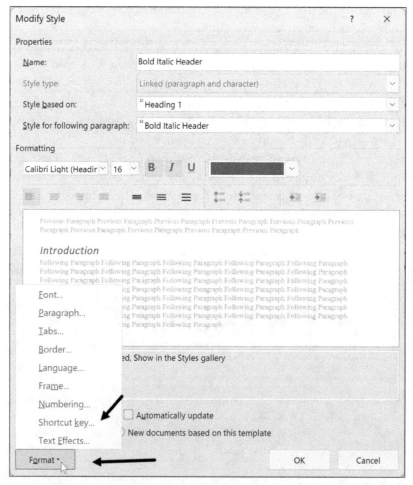

That will open a Customize Keyboard dialogue box where you can click into the Press New Shortcut Key field. Use the shortcut key combination you want and Word will populate it in that field. But watch out that the shortcut you come up with isn't already in use elsewhere. (Word will tell you if it is.)

Here I've assigned Ctrl + } to this style. Word shows that and also shows that it is currently not assigned to any other task:

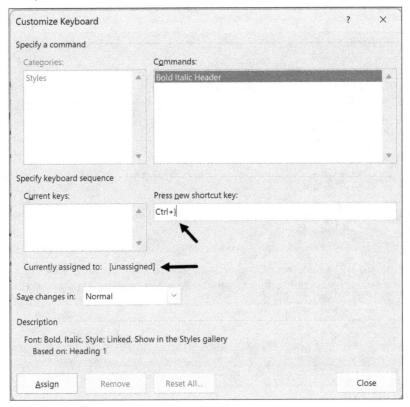

If I want to keep that as my shortcut I can then click on Assign and when I need that format I can apply it to any text in my document using the shortcut instead of having to go to the Style section up top. (It can save time to do this if you're applying styles as you move through a document, because a keyboard shortcut uses the keyboard whereas accessing the menus up top usually requires going to the mouse or trackpad.)

Often, though, what I do is I swap out all of my Normal-formatted paragraphs for paragraphs formatted in my custom style all at once. To do this, right-click on the Normal style option and choose Select All:

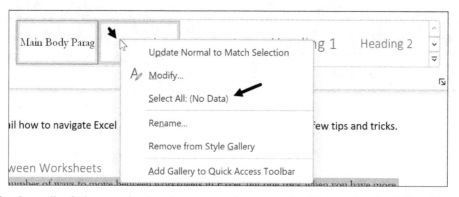

That will select all of the text in the document that uses the Normal style. Like this:

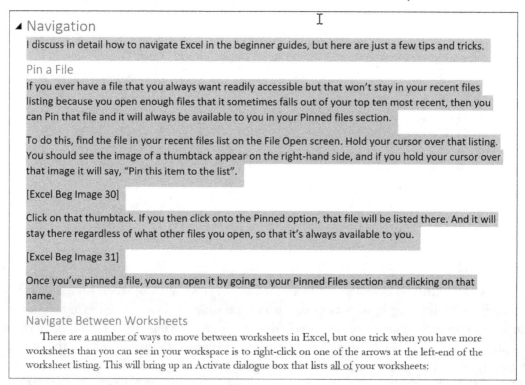

To change all of those Normal-style text entries over to a different style, select the new style from the Styles section. And done:

Navigation

I discuss in detail how to navigate Excel in the beginner guides, but here are just a few tips and tricks.

Pin a File

If you ever have a file that you always want readily accessible but that won't stay in your recent files listing because you open enough files that it sometimes falls out of your top ten most recent, then you can Pin that file and it will always be available to you in your Pinned files section.

To do this, find the file in your recent files list on the File Open screen. Hold your cursor over that listing. You should see the image of a thumbtack appear on the right-hand side, and if you hold your cursor over that image it will say, "Pin this item to the list".

[Excel Beg Image 30]

Click on that thumbtack. If you then click onto the Pinned option, that file will be listed there. And it will stay there regardless of what other files you open, so that it's always available to you.

[Excel Beg Image 31]

Once you've pinned a file, you can open it by going to your Pinned Files section and clicking on that name.

Navigate Between Worksheets

There are a number of ways to move between worksheets in Excel, but one trick when you have more worksheets than you can see in your workspace is to right-click on one of the arrows at the left-end of the worksheet listing. This will bring up an Activate dialogue box that lists all of your worksheets:

It only took about five seconds for Word to apply my new style to all of the paragraphs in my document that had used the Normal style previously. I could do the same for the Heading 1 and Heading 2 styles and then create a first paragraph style that uses a control shortcut and go through and manually apply that one.

A very easy way to format a document.

If you realize that your text style is not formatted the way you want, edit one paragraph of text that uses that style and then right-click on the style name at the top of the workspace and choose Update [Style Name] to Match Selection.

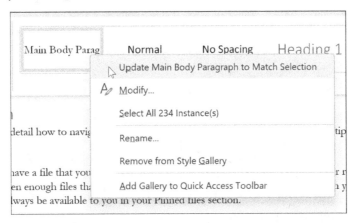

That will change all text entries in your document that use that style.

I find that easier than right-clicking on the style and choosing the Modify option which will open a Modify Style dialogue box where you can change any text or paragraph settings. It works, but it's easier for me to use the Paragraph and Font sections of the Home tab to modify a paragraph instead and then apply my changes that way.

Clicking on the expansion arrow for Styles will open a Styles floating task pane. You can click on Options there to open the Style Pane Options dialogue box which lets you control which styles are shown in the menu as well as a few other settings:

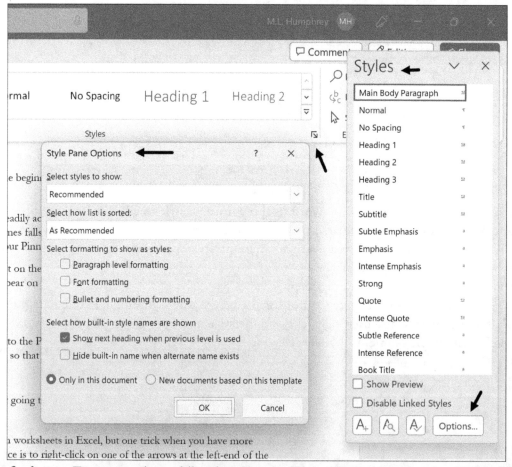

One final note. Every once in a while when I'm working with Heading 1 styles, Word will try to apply them to the paragraph above the chapter name. It's pretty obvious when it happens because you can see the text of that paragraph in the Headings section of the Navigation pane. If that ever happens to you, go to that paragraph, use Enter at the end of the paragraph and then apply the Normal style to it. The chapter name should keep the Heading 1 format, but it won't apply to that paragraph anymore.

And that's it. Pretty simple, but incredibly powerful. You should always use styles that incorporate paragraph formatting and indents instead of trying to use Enters, spaces, and the Tab key to format your text. Trust me on this.

Okay. On to a simple topic now, how to add a watermark to a document.

Watermarks

A watermark is text that appears in the background of a document. It's often light gray in color and says something like "Draft". Watermarks are useful for when you're circulating a document but want to make clear something about that document, like its incomplete status.

To add a watermark to your document, go to the Page Background section of the Design tab and click on the dropdown arrow under Watermark:

The dropdown will give you a few default choices that say CONFIDENTIAL, DO NOT COPY, DRAFT, or SAMPLE. Here are three of those examples:

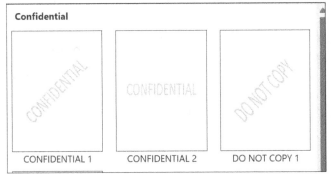

If that works for you, click on the option you want and you're done. The watermark will appear behind your text like this:

To do this, find the file in your recent files list on the File Open screen. Hold your cursor over that listing. You should see the image of a thumbtack appear on the right-hand side, and if you hold your cursor over that image it will say, "Pin this item to the list".

[Excel Beg Image 30]

Click on that thumbtack. If you then click onto the Pinned option, that file will be listed there. And it will stay there regardless of what other files you open, so that it's always available to you.

[Excel Beg Image 31]

Once you've pinned a file, you can open it by going to your Pinned Files section and clicking on that name.

Navigate Between Worksheets

There are a number of ways to move between worksheets in Excel, but one trick when you have more worksheets than you can see in your workspace is to right-click on one of the arrows at the left-end of the worksheet listing. This will bring up an Activate dialogue box that lists all of your worksheets:

[Excel Beg Image 41]

From there click on the name of the worksheet you want and then click on OK and Excel will take you to that worksheet.

Turn Off Scroll Lock

On occasion I will find that navigating in Excel isn't working the way I'm used to. I arrow and things don't move like they should. When this happens, it's usually because Scroll Lock somehow was turned on. The way to turn it back off is to click on the Scroll Lock key on your keyboard.

Unfortunately, I haven't had a computer with a Scroll Lock key in probably a decade, so you have to open a virtual keyboard to do this. Use the Windows key (the one with four squares to the left of your spacebar) + Ctrl + O to open it.

(Another option is to go through your Start menu to Settings and search for keyboard there and then toggle the on-screen keyboard to on.)

The keyboard will appear on your screen and look something like this:

If you don't like those choices, there is an option at the bottom of the dropdown to find more watermarks on Office.com or you can choose Custom Watermark, which will open the Printed Watermark dialogue box.

There you can specify the text, the font, the size of the text, the font color, the transparency level, and the angle of the text. You can also add a picture as your watermark. For the text, there are more options available in that dropdown menu, but you can also click into the box and type your own text.

Here I've changed the watermark to M.L. HUMPHREY and changed the font and color:

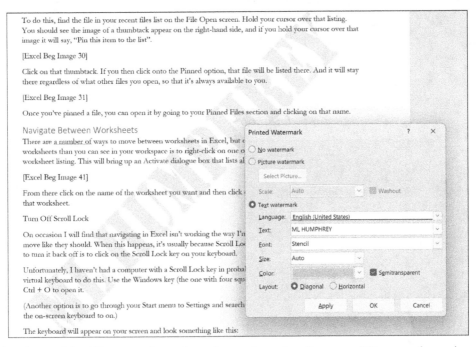

There is also a No Watermark option there, but the Remove Watermark option in the dropdown menu will also remove any watermark that's been added to a document.

If you need to modify an existing watermark, use the Custom Watermark option. You can also replace it by choosing one of the other pre-formatted options.

Page Breaks

It can be tempting to use Enter to move text to the next page when that's needed. Don't. As I've mentioned before and I'll mention again, manually trying to force formatting onto your text is a very, very bad idea. It creates a lot of unnecessary work and is very prone to breaking or having inconsistencies. One little change somewhere in your document and suddenly everything is off.

The way to move text to the next page and not have all those issues is to use a Page Break. To insert one, go to the point in your document where you want to insert the break and then go to the Pages section of the Insert tab and click on Page Break:

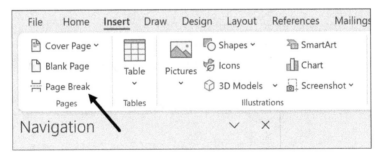

That will automatically move your cursor down to the next page in your document.

By default your page breaks in your document will not be visible. But if you click on the Show/Hide paragraph marks option in the Paragraph section of the Home tab, you can make them visible:

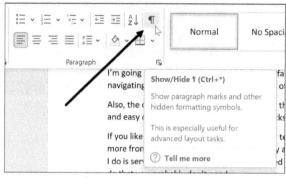

Here is an example of what that looks like:

In this case, the page break is on its own line. Sometimes that can be a problem because it forces a blank page that you don't want. If it is, you can click onto the line above and use Delete to bring the page break up to the last line of text.

If the last line of text is really long, sometimes you'll only see part of the text that identifies a page break:

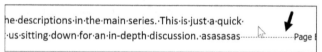

To remove a page break, just treat it like any other text or paragraph mark and either use Delete or Backspace, depending on where you are relative to the break.

You can also find a page break option in the Page Setup section of the Layout tab under the Breaks dropdown menu:

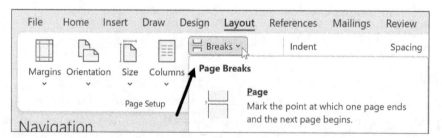

As I mentioned in *Word 365 for Beginners*, Page Break is actually a task that I add to my Quick Access Toolbar so that I don't have to go searching for it since I use it often enough and it's not on the Home tab.

Okay. Now let's discuss section breaks, which can also be found in that Breaks dropdown menu.

Section Breaks

Page breaks simply push text to the next page, but all of the formatting, document size, etc. remains the same. Section breaks, on the other hand, let you create different sections of your document that are formatted in different ways.

When might you need this?

If you are writing a report that has appendices that are landscape orientation instead of portrait orientation, you can achieve this in one single document by using section breaks between the main report and your appendices.

When I used to format print books using Word, I would use section breaks to have different headers and footers in different parts of my book.

So, for example, in the print version of this book you will see that the header for each chapter uses that chapter's name and that there is no header on the page that starts each chapter. The way to achieve that is to have different sections for each chapter.

Another place where that needs to happen is when you have a book that has all chapters starting on the right-hand page which sometimes requires a blank left-hand page. That can only be achieved if the blank page has different headers and footers compared to the other pages in the book.

Also, different sections are needed for any front matter, like tables of contents, which usually have separate page numbering from the main portion of the document.

* * *

Now that you understand what section breaks can be used for, let's look at your available options, which can be found in the Breaks dropdown in the Page Setup section of the Layout tab:

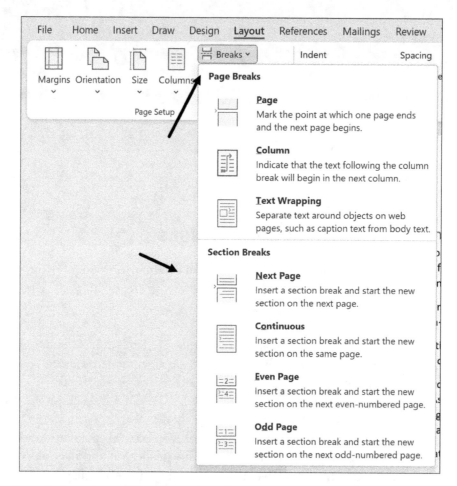

You have four choices there: Next Page, Continuous, Even Page, and Odd Page.

Continuous means that the break will happen on that same page. This could be used for a scenario where you have a single column of text at the top of the page and then multiple columns later in the page. Like this:

• Terminology¶

In·case·any·of·the·terms·I·use·in·this·book·are·unfamiliar·to·you·or·used·in·a·way·that·is·unique·to·me,· here·is·a·brief·run-down·of·terms·you·might·see·in·this·book.·(A·full·discussion·of·each·term·is·covered·in· the·beginner·books,·this·is·just·a·brief·mention.)¶·················Section Break (Continuous)·················

Workbook¶

A·workbook·is·what·Excel·likes·to·call·an·Excel· file.¶

·················Column Break·················

Worksheet¶

Excel·defines·a·worksheet·as·the·primary· document·you·use·in·Excel·to·store·and·work· with·your·data.·A·worksheet·is·organized·into· Columns·and·Rows·that·form·Cells.·A·workbook· can·contain·multiple·worksheets.¶·················

You can see here (maybe) that the first paragraph of that Terminology chapter is a single column. But then below that I have one column with the definition of Workbook next to another column with the definition for Worksheet. There is a Continuous Section Break between that first paragraph and the two definition columns.

When I selected that text and applied two-column formatting to it, Word automatically inserted the Section Break for me, which was nice, but I could have manually inserted it as well. (We'll come back to this more in the next chapter when we cover columns.)

The other three options, Next Page, Even Page, and Odd Page are all options that start a new section on another page. Just as their names imply, that other page is either the next one available, the next even-numbered page, or the next odd-numbered page.

For Even Page and Odd Page, Word will insert a blank page in between if needed.

Now, a warning here. I found in older versions of Word that when I tried to use the Odd Page Break, Word would accurately insert that particular section break, but it would somehow remove my previous odd-page section breaks from my document and turn them into next-page breaks instead.

I no longer use Word for book formatting and I wasn't able to replicate that issue today, so it may be fixed in Word 365 as of January 2023, but in case it isn't, Next Page Breaks always work. They just require a little extra effort if you're trying to have a blank page in there.

What I recommend, and you should do this anyway, is to be sure to check through your entire document when you're done and make sure that everything looks the way you want it. Okay.

Let's walk through this with an actual document that has headers and footers.

First, let's revisit the Headers & Footers Options section. As a reminder, you can add a header and/or footer to a document using the Header & Footer section of the Insert tab. When you do so, a Header & Footer tab will appear and in the Options section of that tab there will be three checkboxes:

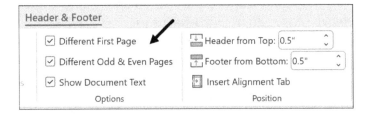

Different First Page is what you need to use when the first page of your document or your section should have a different header and/or footer than the other pages.

Different Odd & Even Pages is what allows you to have different text on the left-hand page and the right-hand page, like in a book where you have author name on one side and book title or chapter title on the other.

Here, I've set it up so that there is no header on the first page, consistent page numbering on the bottom of all pages, and then the even-numbered pages have an author name and the odd-numbered pages have a book title in the header.

To get this to work, I had to add the page numbering to the first page, first even-numbered page, and first odd-numbered page separately.

I zoomed my document to 50% so we can see six pages at once:

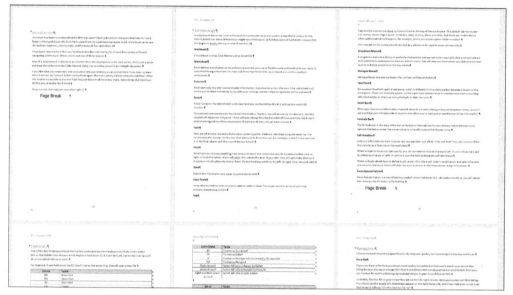

It may be hard to see, but the top of that first page is blank. On the next page, in the header we have the author name. On the next one after that, in the header we have the book title. And then you can see for the next three pages how those alternate in the header between author name and title. Each page where you can see the footer has a page number that goes up by one with each page.

Problem is, that second page is the start of a new chapter, so the header should be blank. Same with the fourth page and sixth page that we can see.

To fix this, each of those pages needs to be the start of a new section.

It is a best practice when adding section breaks to start on page 1 and then work your way through the document and add those breaks as you go. The reason to do this is because as you add breaks the page numbers will shift and that may impact what kind of break you use on later chapters.

Theoretically, if you're using odd-numbered or even-numbered page breaks it won't matter, but for me I prefer to assume I'll have issues and do what I can to avoid them up front.

So I start by going to page 1 and replacing that Page Break with an Odd Page Section Break.

(Be careful that when you replace a Page Break with a Section Break, that you replace it, not add to it. The first time I did this, I highlighted Page Break and then inserted the Section

Break and it kept the Page Break and inserted the Section Break before it. I had to delete the Page Break first and then add the Section Break to get it to work.)

You can see here that now my "second" page also does not have a header, which is what we wanted:

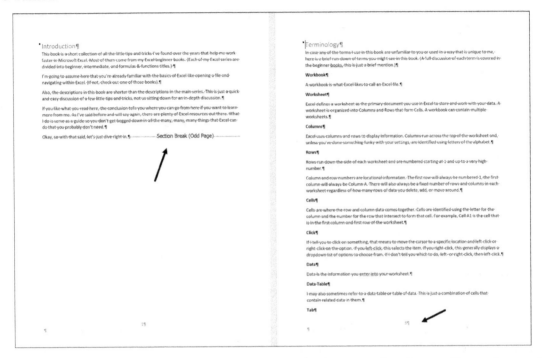

But I want to highlight something here that may be hard to see. That "second" page is actually the third page of the document. Because I used an Odd Page Section Break, Word, behind the scenes, has added a blank page between these two chapters. But it does not show on the screen. Nor does it show in Print Preview.

That blank page will only show up when the document is printed or generated as a PDF. You have to watch out for this because it is not intuitive to realize that there is a page that exists there but is not visible. Here is what that looks like when generated as a PDF:

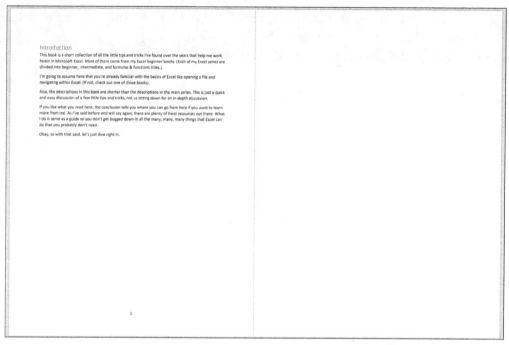

I can now walk through the rest of my document and replace my page breaks with section breaks. I want to have each chapter start on an odd-numbered page, so I will use the Odd Page Section Break.

Word carries through the header and footer settings from the original document, so each new chapter has a blank first page header and then uses the author name and book title on the even- and odd-numbered pages, respectively. Each page is also numbered at the bottom.

For this book here, as written, that would be the end of it. But let's change things up a bit. I combined a few of my chapters so I'd have enough pages in each chapter to see the book title at the top of the page. Here are six pages from the middle of the book across two "chapters":

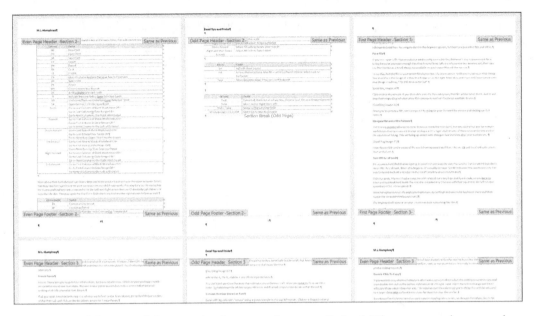

The headers and footers right now in these sections are linked. That means that any change I make to any of those headers or footers will carry over between the sections. For example, I just bolded the text in the headers for those first two pages and that bolding carried over to the bottom three pages.

But if you're trying to use different text at the top of a page for a section, you don't want that. The way to unlink your sections is to go to the Navigation section of the Header & Footer tab and unselect the Link to Previous option.

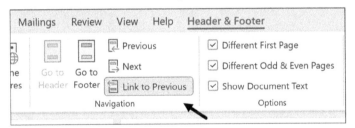

This is selected by default. Click into the second of the linked headers or footers first before you choose to unlink a header or footer since the option is to link to *previous*. Once you've unlinked your section from the prior section, you can edit the header or footer and it will not impact the prior section's header or footer.

If you are transitioning between front matter, like a table of contents, to the main body of your document or from the main body of your document to a standalone appendix, or using your chapter names for the header text, then you will need to do this.

I often find that I forget about this and make a change and then have to go back and unlink sections and then fix the one I inadvertently changed.

In my experience, working with section breaks and different headers and footers between those sections can take a little bit of trial and error to get everything to work properly. This is usually more about figuring out what should or should not be linked and making changes where they need to be made, but sometimes it seems to me that Word is more prone to do weird things the more complex your document becomes. So, don't get discouraged. Just fix things as they break and sometimes maybe find a simpler option (like a Next Page break instead of an Odd or Even Page break.)

Columns and Column Breaks

Since we just touched on it briefly above, I'm going to take a quick minute here and tell you how to change your document so that it has multiple columns of text on a single page.

First step, select your text that you want to place into multiple columns. Next, go to the Page Setup section of the Layout tab and click on the dropdown arrow below Columns.

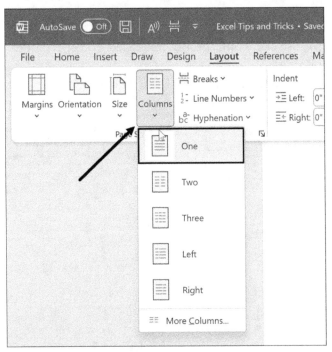

Choose your desired number of columns from the dropdown, which gives the option of one, two, or three columns as well as an option that has a skinnier left or right column next to a larger column.

If none of those options work for you, click on the More Columns option to bring up the Columns dialogue box:

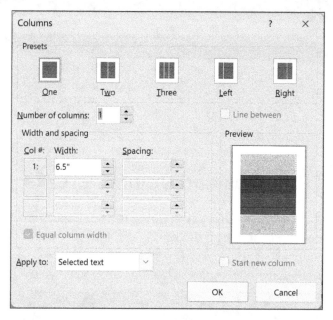

The dialogue box has those same options, but it also lets you specify different column widths for each column if you want.

You can also put a line between your columns if you want, like I've done here:

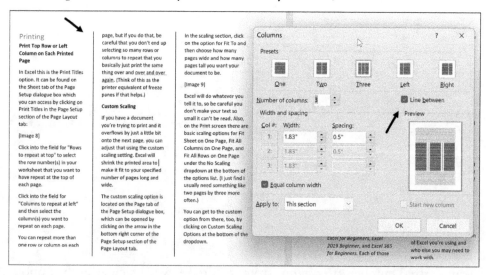

When you apply columns to a text selection, the default is for Word to spread that text evenly across the desired number of columns. Like so:

Workbook¶

A·workbook·is·what·Excel· likes·to·call·an·Excel·file.¶

Worksheet¶

Excel·defines·a·worksheet·as· the·primary·document·you· use·in·Excel·to·store·and· work·with·your·data.·A· worksheet·is·organized·into· Columns·and·Rows·that·form· Cells.·A·workbook·can· contain·multiple·worksheets.¶

Columns¶

Excel·uses·columns·and·rows· to·display·information.· Columns·run·across·the·top· of·the·worksheet·and,·unless· you've·done·something·funky· with·your·settings,·are· identified·using·letters·of·the· alphabet.¶

Rows¶

Rows·run·down·the·side·of· each·worksheet·and·are· numbered·starting·at·1·and· up·to·a·very·high·number.¶

Column·and·row·numbers· are·locational·information.·

The·first·row·will·always·be· numbered·1,·the·first·column· will·always·be·Column·A.· There·will·also·always·be·a· fixed·number·of·rows·and· columns·in·each·worksheet· regardless·of·how·many·rows· of·data·you·delete,·add,·or· move·around.¶

Cells¶

Cells·are·where·the·row·and· column·data·comes·together.· Cells·are·identified·using·the· letter·for·the·column·and·the· number·for·the·row·that· intersect·to·form·that·cell.· For·example,·Cell·A1·is·the· cell·that·is·in·the·first·column· and·first·row·of·the· worksheet.¶

Click¶

If·I·tell·you·to·click·on· something,·that·means·to· move·the·cursor·to·a·specific· location·and·left-click·or· right-click·on·the·option.·If· you·left-click,·this·selects·the· item.·If·you·right-click,·this· generally·displays·a· dropdown·list·of·options·to·

choose·from.·If·I·don't·tell· you·which·to·do,·left-·or· right-click,·then·left-click.¶

Data¶

Data·is·the·information·you· enter·into·your·worksheet.¶

Data·Table¶

I·may·also·sometimes·refer· to·a·data·table·or·table·of· data.·This·is·just·a· combination·of·cells·that· contain·related·data·in·them.¶

Tab¶

Tabs·are·the·options·you· have·to·choose·from·at·the· top·of·the·workspace.·The· default·tab·names·are·File,· Home,·Insert,·Page·Layout,· Formulas,·Data,·Review,· View,·and·Help.·But·there·are· certain·times·when· additional·tabs·will·appear,· for·example,·when·you· create·a·pivot·table·or·a· chart.¶

(This·should·not·be·confused· with·the·Tab·key·which·can· be·used·to·move·across· cells.)¶·Section Break (Continuous)·

Here I've taken a text selection and placed the text into three columns. If you read the entries, the text goes all the way down the first column and then continues to the second and then to the third. But because it's a selection, the amount of text in each column is about the same.

If you apply columns to an entire document instead, it will fill the first column on the page and then move on to the next column and then the next. In situations where there isn't enough text to fill the page you end up with something like this:

See how on the left-hand page there are only two columns with text in them and how on the right-hand page there are only two lines of text in the last column but the other two columns are full?

To balance the text across a page, click at the very end of the text on that page and then apply a Continuous Section Break. (Page Setup section of the Layout tab, Breaks dropdown, Section Breaks, Continuous.) Your result will look something like this:

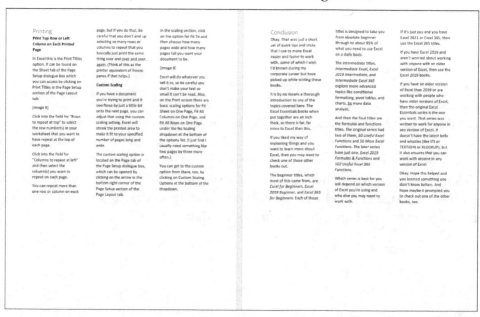

As mentioned above in the chapter on section breaks, if you add columns to a selection of text in your document, Word will automatically add the Continuous Section Breaks for you at the start and at the end of the selection.

Sometimes where the text falls naturally is not going to be what you want. Like here:

Workbook A workbook is what Excel likes to call an Excel file. **Worksheet**	Excel defines a worksheet as the primary document you use in Excel to store and work with your data. A worksheet is organized into Columns and Rows that form Cells. A workbook can contain multiple worksheets.

I put these entries into two columns, but the problem is that "Worksheet" naturally falls at the bottom of the left-hand column when it would be better placed at the top of the right-hand column.

You can force the text to break at a different point by inserting a Column Break. To do so, click where you need the break and then go to the Page Setup section of the Layout Tab and choose Column from the Breaks dropdown menu.

Much better:

Workbook A workbook is what Excel likes to call an Excel file.	**Worksheet** Excel defines a worksheet as the primary document you use in Excel to store and work with your data. A worksheet is organized into Columns and Rows that form Cells. A workbook can contain multiple worksheets.

Okay, so that was columns and column breaks. Now on to tables.

Tables

When I was in a corporate job we used tables all the time, so this is one that's definitely worth mastering. But if you really want to be good with tables you not only need to be able to insert them into a document, you need to format them properly, too, so this is going to be a long chapter.

Insert

To insert a table, go to the Insert tab and click on the dropdown for Table in the Tables section:

Under that Insert Table section, you can hold your mouse over the number of rows and columns you want in your table and Word will draw that for you in the document. Like so:

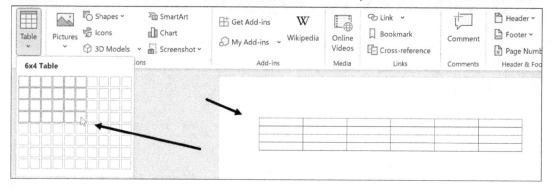

Click to insert the table.

Don't worry so much about the number of rows, but it is nice to start with the proper number of columns. (To add new rows to a table you can just go to the last cell in the table and use the Tab key and Word will add another row, so especially if you're directly entering the values in the table, the number of rows is easy to fix as needed.)

If you click on Insert Table in that dropdown instead, it will open the Insert Table dialogue box which lets you specify a number for columns and rows and also specify the AutoFit behavior for the table (fixed width, fit to contents, fit to window).

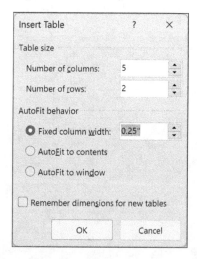

Another option is the Draw Table option, which is located in that same dropdown menu. It basically lets you left-click and drag to place a rectangle and then left-click and drag to draw lines within it, but I never use that option myself.

The Quick Tables option is another one I don't use. It inserts a pre-formatted table template.

The Excel Spreadsheet option will embed a working Excel spreadsheet into your document that displays as a table. When you're working in that one, your interface up top will actually be the Excel interface. But when you click away it will look like an ordinary table. Double-click on the table to get back into the Excel interface.

For working with calculations, the Excel Spreadsheet option is probably a better choice than trying to work directly in Word, but all of your formatting of that table will have to happen in the Excel interface, because once you close the interface Word will treat the table as a picture that can't be formatted or edited.

For this book we're just going to stick to a basic table.

When you insert a normal table in Word, you will see two new tabs appear at the top of the workspace, Table Design and Layout. There are a number of formatting choices you can make there, but first I just want to talk about a basic table using the Home tab options.

Here I've inserted a table in my document:

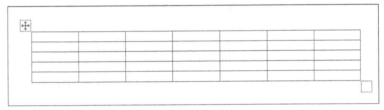

Now let's walk through how to add text and format that table.

Add Text

To input text into the table, you can click into a cell and type. Use the Tab key to move to the next cell in a row or Shift + Tab to move back one cell. If you're at the end of a row, it will move you to the next cell on the row below or above, depending on which direction you were moving.

If you have data to paste into your table, select all of the cells in the table first that will contain that data and then paste (Ctrl + V or one of the paste special options). If you don't select cells first, the data will all paste into that one cell where your cursor was. If you select less than the required number of cells, only the data for those cells will paste in. If you select too many cells, the data will paste in more than once to fill the selected number of cells.

Delete Text

To delete the text in a specific cell, select that text and then use the Backspace or Delete key. If you need to delete text in more than one cell at a time, use the Delete key.

If you select text in more than one cell or select an entire cell and try to use the Backspace key, Excel will want to also delete the cell not just the text. You'll see a Delete Cells dialogue box appear. You can close that box if that wasn't your intent, or choose one of the listed options if that was what you wanted to do.

Delete Contents of Table

To delete the contents of the entire table, click on the white box with four arrows in the top left corner of the table and then use the Delete key.

Delete Table

To delete the entire table, click on the white box with four arrows in the top left corner of the table and then use the Backspace key.

You can also use Cut once the table is selected or go to the Rows & Columns section of the table Layout tab, use the Delete dropdown menu, and choose Delete Table.

Format Text

You can format any text in a table just like you would other text. Select the cell(s) you want to format and then use the Font section of the Home tab or Ctrl shortcuts to apply your formatting. There are also alignment and text direction options in the Alignment section of the Layout tab.

Shading

One type of formatting that we didn't discuss in *Word 365 for Beginners* is Shading. That's because I usually only use it for tables. I like to have the first row of a table use a shaded background behind my text. Like so:

Value	Decimal Places	ROUND	ROUNDUP	ROUNDDOWN
3.124	2	3.12	3.13	3.12
3.126	2	3.13	3.13	3.12
-3.1246	2	-3.12	-3.13	-3.12
-3.1262	2	-3.13	-3.13	-3.12

That lets me distinguish my labels from my data.

To apply shading, select those cell(s), and then go to the Paragraph section of the Home tab. The Shading option is in the bottom row on the right-hand side. It looks like a paint bucket tilted to the right.

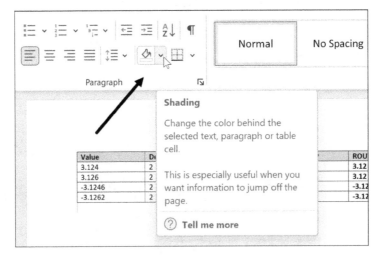

Click on the dropdown arrow to see the available color choices:

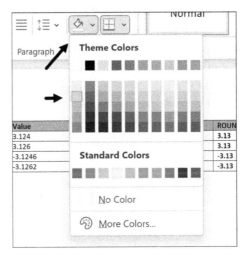

There are seventy colors there to choose from, but if you need a different color you can click on More Colors to open the Color dialogue box. The No Color option is what to use to remove shading from your selected cell(s).

There is also a Shading option in the Table Styles section of the Table Design tab as well as in the mini formatting menu.

Borders

By default, when you insert a table in Word it will have a border around all four sides of each cell. If you want to remove or edit the style of one of those borders, you can use the Borders dropdown in the Paragraph section of the Home tab:

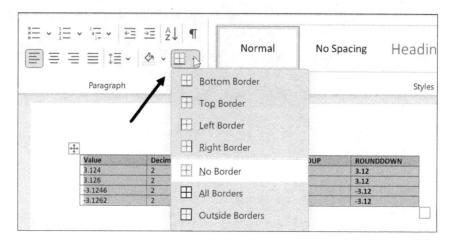

The borders that are currently applied to the table will be shaded in gray. The borders that are not currently in use will be unshaded. Hold your mouse over each option to see what the table will look like if that border is removed or added. Click to apply that change.

If you click on the Borders and Shading option at the bottom of the dropdown menu, that will open the Borders and Shading dialogue box which will let you change the line width, style, or color. Make those changes before applying new borders to your table.

Choose the Custom setting and use the Preview section to choose which lines to change if you want to use more than one line style, width, or color in your table at a time.

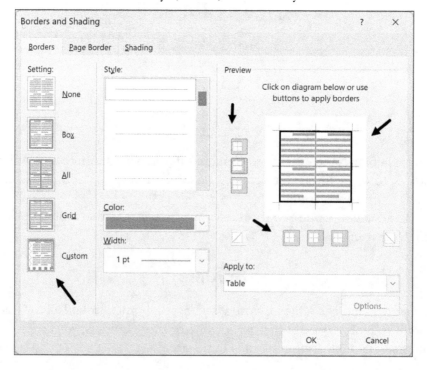

You can also select just a subset of the cells in the table to format those differently if needed, like I did here for the top row of this table which needed a different cell border than the main cells in the table:

Value	Decimal Places	ROUND	ROUNDUP	ROUNDDOWN
3.124	2	3.12	3.13	3.12
3.126	2	3.13	3.13	3.12
-3.1246	2	-3.12	-3.13	-3.12
-3.1262	2	-3.13	-3.13	-3.12

The Table Design tab also has a Borders section where you can choose your line style, line weight, and line color. If you make all of your selections there, you can then use the Border Painter and click on individual lines within your table to change their formatting:

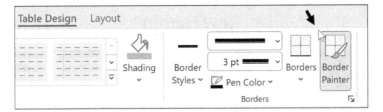

There is also a Borders dropdown menu there, but if you want to use it be sure to select the whole table or the cells you want to format first before making your selection.

You can also right-click on your table and choose Border Styles from the dropdown menu there to choose from a selection of twenty-one line styles which you can then apply one cell border at a time by clicking on the cell border.

Column Width

To manually adjust the width of a column in a table, left-click on the right-hand or left-hand border for that column and then hold that left-click and drag:

Value	Decimal Places	ROUND
3.124	2	3.12
3.126	2	3.13
-3.1246	2	-3.12
-3.1262	2	-3.13

(If you have your cursor positioned in the right spot it will turn into two vertical lines with arrows pointing in either direction.)

If you click and drag in the direction of another column, it will also change the width of the neighboring column so that the total width of the two columns combined remains the same. If you click and drag from the outer perimeter of the first or last column in the table, it will change the overall width of the table.

You can also right-click and choose to Distribute Columns Evenly or you can click on Distribute Columns in the Cell Size section of the Layout tab if you want all of your columns to be the same width.

Another option is to right-click on the column and choose Table Properties from the dropdown menu. Go to the Column tab and choose a new value for the Preferred Width of that column.

Or you can go to the table Layout tab and change the value for Width under Cell Size.

Both of those last two options will change the overall width of the table as well.

I will often combine the left-click and drag option on the first or last column to change the overall width of the table and then use that Distribute Columns option to fix the width of the columns based on the new table width.

Row Height

As you type text into a cell in Word the height of that row will automatically adjust so that all of the text is visible. (See image below for an example.) It is not possible to change a row height to hide any text in that row.

But you can left-click and drag along the upper or lower border of a cell to change the row height so that there's more space than the text takes up. (The cursor will look like two parallel lines with arrows pointing up and down when you have it positioned correctly.)

Value and then a lot of text to give this a new height	Decimal Places	ROUND	ROUNDUP	ROUNDDOWN
3.124	2	3.12	3.13	3.12
3.126	2	3.13	3.13	3.12
-3.1246	2	-3.12	-3.13	-3.12
-3.1262	2	-3.13	-3.13	-3.12

You can also open the Table Properties dialogue box or change the Height value in the Cell Size section of the table Layout tab.

If you choose Distribute Rows in the table Layout tab or Distribute Rows Evenly by right-clicking, that will resize your rows so that they are all the same size based upon the cell that is the tallest. Like here where all rows are now the height of the header row:

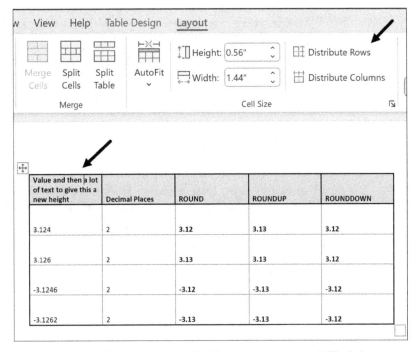

Space Between Cells or Around Table

To add space between cells or around the perimeter of your table, use the Cell Margins option in the Alignment section of the Layout tab to open the Table Options dialogue box.

Changing the value for Default Cell Spacing will add a space between the cells in each row and column. You can see that in the image below where each cell of the table is separated from the other cells in the table:

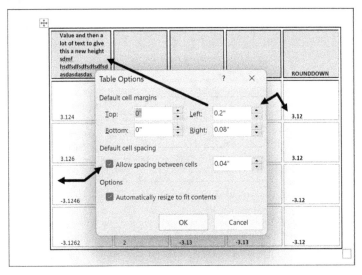

Adjusting the Default Cell Margins values adds space between the borders of each cell and the text within the cells.

You can see an example of this in the left-hand cell in the column header row where the text is indented from the left-hand side by .2" and from the right-hand side by only .08". Note how the text in that cell is visibly closer to the right-hand side of the cell.

Repeat Header Row

If you have a table that stretches across more than one page, then you will likely want to have the header row for that table on both pages. Rather than try to manually do that, which you should not do, there is an option that allows you to repeat the header row.

This is available in the Data section of the table Layout tab. Click on the option there.

Or you can right-click and choose Table Properties to open the Table Properties dialogue box and then go to the Row tab and check the box there.

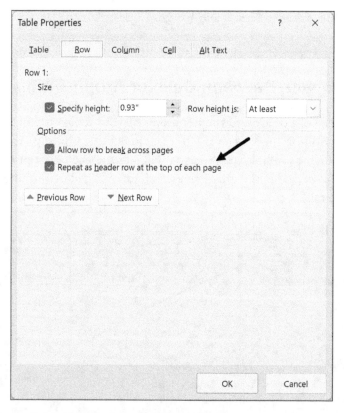

That option is only available for the first row of the table.

Insert Rows or Columns

We already discussed how to add an extra row to the end of a table. Just use Tab from the last cell in the table and Word will automatically add another row. But sometimes you will want to add a row(s) or column(s) in the midst of a table. Click on that location and then you have two options.

The first option is the Rows & Columns section of the table Layout tab:

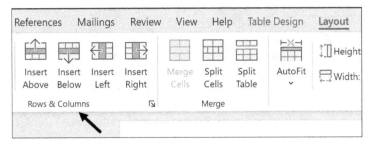

But I usually just right-click on the table and choose Insert from the dropdown menu and then my desired option from that secondary dropdown menu:

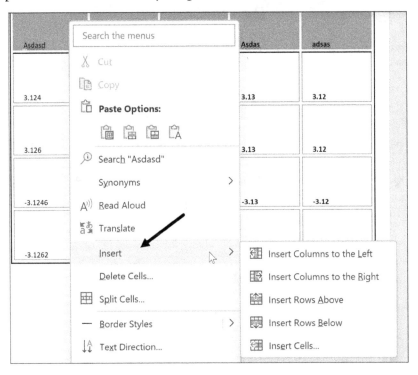

Note that if you insert columns that will change the overall width of your table so you may have to make adjustments after doing so to get the table to fit on the page again.

Delete Rows or Columns

To delete a column or row in a table, right-click on a cell in the column or row you want to delete and then choose the Delete option from the dropdown menu. This will bring up the Delete Cells dialogue box where you can choose to delete the entire row or column.

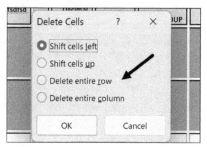

Your other option is to use the Delete dropdown menu in the Rows & Columns section of the Layout tab. Or to select one or more cells in that row or column and then use the Backspace key to bring up the Delete Cells dialogue box.

Delete Cell(s)

I don't recommend doing this, but it is possible to delete a single cell in a table using the above options.

Resize Table

To resize a table, right-click, choose Table Properties from the dropdown menu, and then go to the Table tab of the Table Properties dialogue box and change the value for Preferred Width. Click on OK. This will change your column widths, so you will probably have to adjust those afterward.

(The other option, mentioned above, is to resize a column at one end or the other of your table.)

Move Table

To move a table, left-click on the square with four arrows in the top left corner of the table and then drag.

Split Table

To split your table into two separate tables, click into the row that you want to be the first row in the second table and then go to the Merge section of the table Layout tab and click on Split Table.

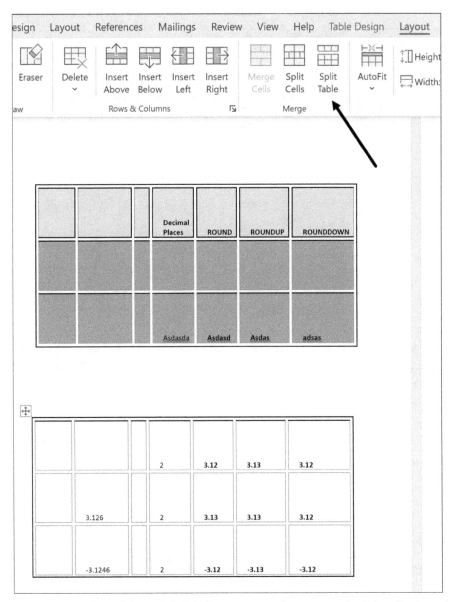

For whatever reason, when I just did this in my own document, it did split the tables but it placed them on top of one another, so I had to move one of the tables down to see both of them. (I don't recall it doing this in the past so I may have done something funky to cause that, but in case you do the same, that's how to fix it.)

Split Cells

You can split a cell in a table into multiple cells using the Split Cells option in the Merge section of the table Layout tab. Clicking on that option opens the Split Cells dialogue box which will let you specify a number of columns and rows for your split.

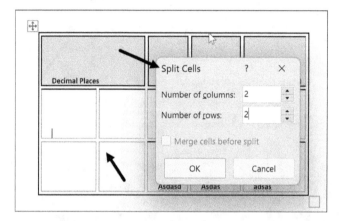

I believe I have used this before when I wanted to have a label row that covered more than one column, like Decimal Places now does above those two columns. But I may have also used Merge Cells for that instead.

This one is weird if there is already text in those cells. If you choose Merge Cells Before Split, it seems to bring that text up to the first X entries where X is the number of original cells in your selection. Otherwise, it puts the text in the left-most cell and doesn't let you split cells across rows. Best to do this before there's text involved.

Also, when you fill in the Split Cells dialogue box, the number of rows is the total number of rows for your selection, so if you selected two rows' worth of cells but then put 1 for the Number of Rows, that would actually merge those cells.

Merge Cells

To merge cells in a table, select the cells you want to merge and then use the Merge Cells option in the Merge section of the table Layout tab. It will automatically merge all of those cells and combine their contents into multiple rows of text within the cell.

Table Styles and Table Style Options

Finally, the Table Design tab has a number of Table Styles that are pre-formatted table style options:

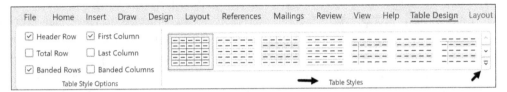

Click on the downpointing arrow with a line above it to see all of them:

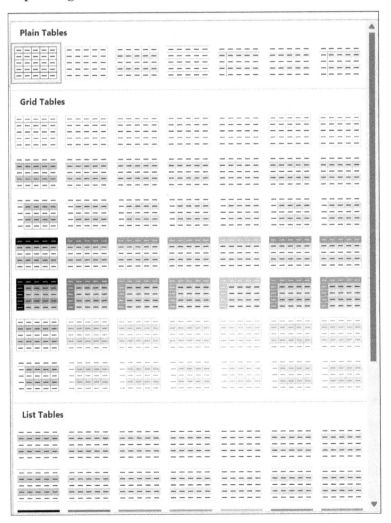

You'll have to use your scroll bar on the right-hand side to see the last few.

Click on any of those styles to apply it to your table. If you don't want to use the header row, first column, total row, last column, banded rows, or banded columns portion of the style, you can uncheck the box for that option in the Table Style Options section.

Or if you want to add that type of formatting, you can check those boxes.

As you check and uncheck those boxes the table styles will update to reflect how those changes will impact your table format. If the style has already been applied to your table, the table will also update.

I personally don't use table styles because they're never what I want so I just stick to a plain table style and then add my own shading as needed, but this is a way to get banded rows which can sometimes be useful. Just choose the Plain Table 1 option and uncheck Banded Columns if it's checked.

Symbols

To insert a symbol or character into your text, put your cursor where you want that symbol or character inserted and then go to the Symbols section of the Insert tab and click on the dropdown arrow. The dropdown will show twenty common symbols by default:

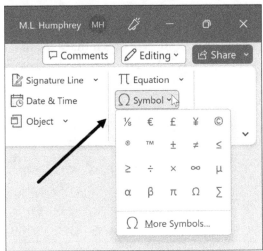

If you want one of those, click on it. (As you work in Word that list of symbols will change to reflect any symbols or characters you've used so that your most-recently-used symbols will be readily available to you.)

If you want a different character or symbol, then click on the More Symbols option to open the Symbol dialogue box.

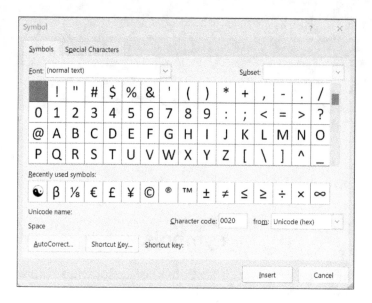

Sixteen common or recently-used symbols will display in a row towards the bottom of the dialogue box. But above that is a large area with sixty-four symbols visible. It has a scroll bar on the right-hand side that you can use to move through all available characters and symbols.

However, I usually like to use that Font dropdown that's located above the visible symbols to choose the font I want to use. The Wingdings fonts tend to have the most shapes available, for example:

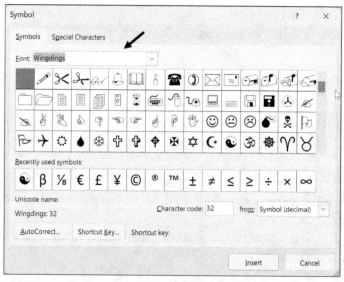

If you use a specific character or symbol often enough, you can create a keyboard shortcut for it by clicking on the Shortcut Key option at the bottom of the dialogue box and then assigning a shortcut using the Customize Keyboard dialogue box.

Many of the non-American-English letters already have shortcuts available that you can see in the bottom of the dialogue box when you select them:

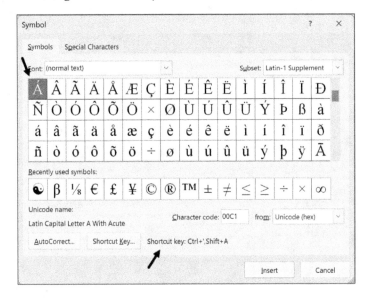

There is also a Special Characters tab that includes grammar marks and common symbols like the copyright and trademark symbols. Many of these also have keyboard shortcuts that are shown with them:

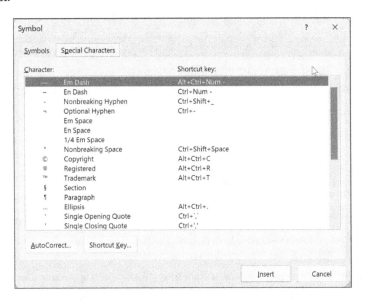

Some also have AutoCorrect options. If you click on that AutoCorrect button at the bottom, it will open the AutoCorrect dialogue box where you can see them:

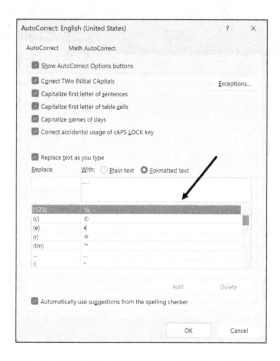

In this screenshot there are listings for the copyright, trademark, and registered symbols as well as the Euro symbol.

Once a symbol or character has been inserted into your document, it's treated like text. You can delete it just like you would any other text and also apply font size, color, bold, etc.

For special characters, as you change the font, the character may also change to match that font. For example, the copyright symbol looks different in different fonts. But shapes, like ones from the Wingdings fonts, will remain unchanged.

Here I've inserted five shapes or characters and then applied four different fonts to them:

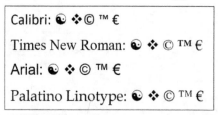

You can see that the first two Wingdings shapes remain unchanged, but that the C in the copyright symbol changes as does the TM in the trademark symbol. And that the Euro symbol is different between all four.

Which is a reminder, too, that if you copy a symbol from another document, be sure to paste it in with the Keep Text Only option so that it uses the font of your document.

Okay, that was symbols, now I want to touch very briefly on all the other things you can insert into a document.

Pictures and Shapes

In the Illustrations section of the Insert tab there are seven types of illustrations you can insert into your document: Pictures, Shapes, Icons, 3D Models, SmartArt, Chart, and Screenshot.

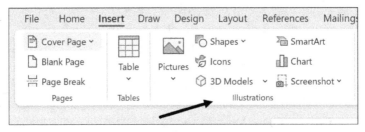

In this chapter we'll cover two of the most popular of those options, Pictures and Shapes.

Pictures

The Pictures option lets you insert a picture into your document.

The picture can either be one you have stored on your computer (or an external device like a thumb drive) or it can be one that comes from online pictures or stock images. If you want to insert a picture from OneDrive, use the Online Pictures option and change the dropdown from Bing to OneDrive.

If you use online pictures or stock images, be sure that you have the right to do so. It can be very costly to use an image you don't have the rights to and it's best to get into the habit of only using images that you either took yourself or have paid to use.

Here we're just going to walk through how to use the first option in the Pictures dropdown menu, Insert Picture From This Device.

When you choose that option, an Insert Picture dialogue box will appear that allows you to locate an image to insert. Navigate to where you have the image stored, click on it, and then click on Insert.

When you do so, the image will come into your document at a default size related to its overall properties and the size of your document.

A Picture Format tab will appear that lets you change the color settings, apply borders, change the image size, and adjust how the picture is positioned relative to your text or other objects:

To change the size of a picture, I recommend using the Size section of the Picture Format tab. By default the aspect ratio for your picture should be locked which means that if you change width or height it will adjust the other measurement as well to keep the image proportionate.

There are also white circles around the perimeter of an inserted image that you can left-click on and drag to resize an image, but be careful with pictures because if you do so from one of the sides, you can distort the image.

To delete an image, select it and then use the Delete or Backspace key.

Shapes

The Shapes option allows you to insert a variety of shapes into your document.

Click on the dropdown arrow next to Shapes to choose the shape you want. Here is the top part of that dropdown menu, but there are many more options.

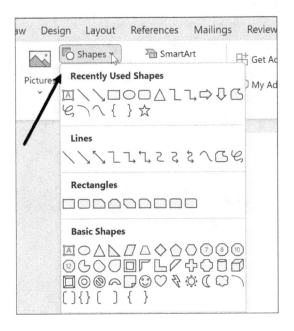

Click on the shape you want and then left-click and drag to insert the shape into your workspace.

When you create a shape there will be a Shape Format dialogue box that allows you to control color, size, and position relative to other objects and text in your document.

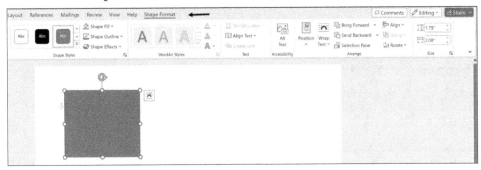

You can also make changes directly to the shape. Left-click on the white circles around the perimeter of a shape and then drag to change the size of the shape. Left-click on the yellow circles (when available) to change the shape itself. The little circle with an arrow at the top (when available) will allow you to rotate the shape.

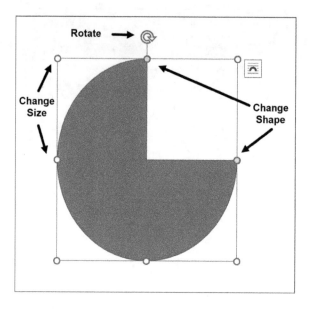

Click away from the shape to return to your text or other objects.

Formatting and Placement

As mentioned above, there will be a special Format tab that appears when you insert a Picture or Shape. The Styles menu has pre-formatted appearance settings and then to the right of that are more specific effects and formatting options.

The Position dropdown allows you to specify how the picture or shape should sit relative to your text.

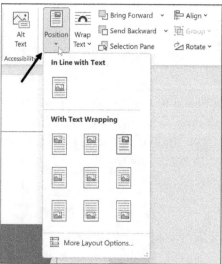

Each option has a visual representation that shows how the object will be positioned relative to your text. Click on More Layout Options to have more control over your object placement and how that object moves or relates to your text.

The Wrap Text dropdown specifies how text will interact with the object and, again, each choice has a small image that visually represents how that would look:

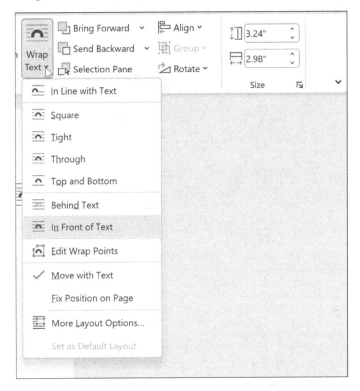

The other options in the Arrange section of each Format tab allow you to specify how different objects will interact with one another. You can specify which will be visible when two objects overlap or choose how to align objects either to one another or to the page.

Other Illustrations and Equations (Brief)

Now let us cover the remaining illustration types very briefly as well as equations.

Other Illustrations

The other options in the Illustrations section of the Insert tab are Icons, 3D Models, SmartArt, Chart, and Screenshot. They work much like Pictures or Shapes in the sense that you choose the one you want and insert it and then can use a Format tab to change attributes.

Icons

Icons require an internet connection before you can insert them in Word 365. They are stock images that are black line drawings of a variety of items like sunglasses, alarm clocks, apples, etc. When you click on this option you also have the ability to choose Cutout People, Stickers, Illustrations, and Cartoon People.

3D Models

3D Models are 3D images that you can insert into your document, some of which are animated. You can use the circle with rotating lines in the middle of the model when inserted to rotate up, down, or to the side.

SmartArt

SmartArt are various illustrative graphics that you can insert into Word that demonstrate processes, cycles, hierarchies, relationships, etc. You choose the graphic that you want to use and then can add your own values to that graphic.

When you insert one into your document a Type Your Text Here dialogue box should appear that lets you input those values. If you close the dialogue box the Text Pane option in the Create Graphic section of the SmartArt Design tab will bring it back up.

I discuss this more in the PowerPoint books, but just be careful when choosing SmartArt that the visual representation actually matches your values. I once saw someone, for example, using a pyramid SmartArt object for unrelated data. Don't do that. Your chosen visual should support the data not contradict it.

Chart

The Chart option will allow you to choose a type of chart to insert into your document. When you do so, there will be an Excel data table that appears on the screen where you can add the values that will build the chart. If you close that window and need to edit those values, use the Edit Data dropdown in the Chart Design tab to bring it back.

Screenshot

The screenshot option lets you take a screenshot of any of the other programs you have open on your computer. If you use the Screen Clipping option you can click and drag to select a subset of that image.

Equations

Directly above the Symbols option in the Symbols section of the Insert tab is an option for Equation that has a dropdown menu available:

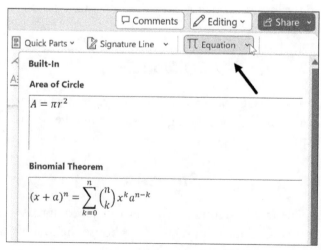

If you click on one of the listed equations, Word will insert that equation as shown into your document in a separate input box like it did here for Area of Circle:

You can choose a format for the equation that is either Professional or Linear. The image above uses a professional format where there is a superscript used for the 2. In linear that would show as ^2 instead and everything would be on one line.

Click on the dots on the left-hand side of that input box and drag to reposition the equation in your document.

If you want to create a custom equation, click on Equation in the Insert tab instead of using the dropdown menu. That will insert a blank box that says Type Equation Here and then you can use the Symbols and Structures sections of the Equation tab to build your equation:

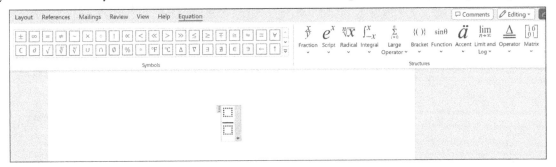

Above, I chose one of the options from the Fractions dropdown under the Structures section. I can now click on each of those dotted boxes and add numbers or symbols to build out the equation.

To delete an equation, select it by clicking on the dots on the left-hand side and then use the Backspace key. You can also use Cut to remove it once it's been selected.

MultiLevel Lists

Time for one of the most annoying topics I wanted to cover in this book, multilevel lists.

Why are they so annoying? If you use them as-is and for the entire document, they're not. But if you try to customize them it can be very painful. Same with if you try to use them in addition to other lists in the same document.

Also, last I checked, they need customization because they don't follow a standard format. The one I'm going to show you here, for example, is fine for the first three levels, but then uses an a with a paren instead of an a with a period, which is not how I was taught it should go.

But let's go look, shall we.

Multilevel lists can be found in the Paragraph section of the Home tab in the top row next to bulleted lists and numbered lists which were already covered in *Word 365 for Beginner*s:

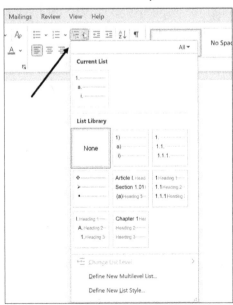

The list choice that's closest to what I was raised with in school is that third one down on the left in the list library, so I'm going to select it and then create a few entries.

Here's what I came up with:

> I.   This is the main level entry for this <u>topic</u>
> **This is me adding text below that point.**
>
>   A.   Now I want a sub-entry.
>
>   B.   And another sub-entry.
>
>   ◢ 1.   And a subpoint of that one.

A few points to mention here that are important.

With a bulleted or numbered list, when you hit Enter the next line is automatically also bulleted or numbered. With a multilevel list, that is not the case. The next line is text.

Furthermore, that text is not indented. The cursor goes back each time to the far left-hand side of the page.

Using the Tab key will get you to a point directly below the text in the prior line so you can add a description or paragraph like I did above under the first main point.

For those other entries, the A, the B, and the 1, I had to go up to the Paragraph section of the Home tab, click on the dropdown for Multilevel List, and then click on the current list I was using.

If your cursor is not already indented to the level you want, place the cursor before the text in that line and use the Tab key to move the text one indent level at a time.

Another option for getting the right list level is to go back to that dropdown and use the Change List Level option to choose the desired list level.

You can also use the Indent options in the Paragraph section of the Home tab.

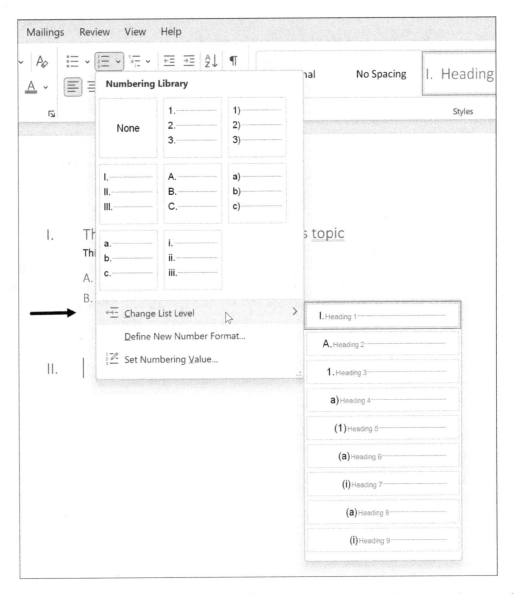

Each list level will have a black arrow that will appear to the left of the entry when you hold your mouse over it that you can click on to hide everything below that entry.

The nice thing about the multilevel list is that it does continue throughout your document even if there is text in between. So if I type text and then add a new multilevel list entry after that text, it will continue the numbering from above:

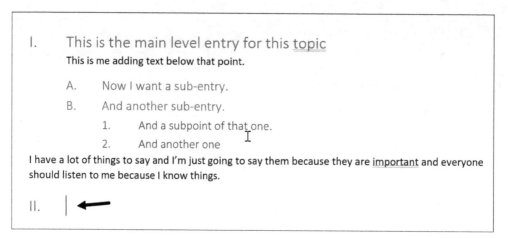

If the default numbering options don't work for you, you can choose Define New Multilevel List from the multilevel list dropdown to create your own list. That will open the Define New Multilevel List dialogue box where you can then for each level choose the number formatting to use, the alignment for the number, and the amount the text should be indented.

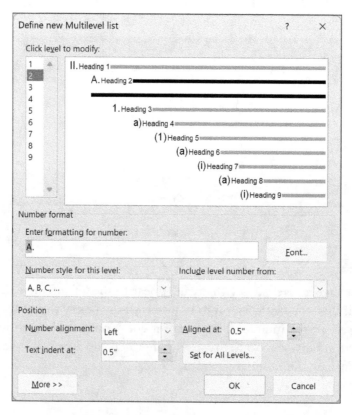

Click on More to see more options such as how to separate the number from the text (default is a Tab character) and where to apply those changes and what numbering to start at and when to restart that level's numbering.

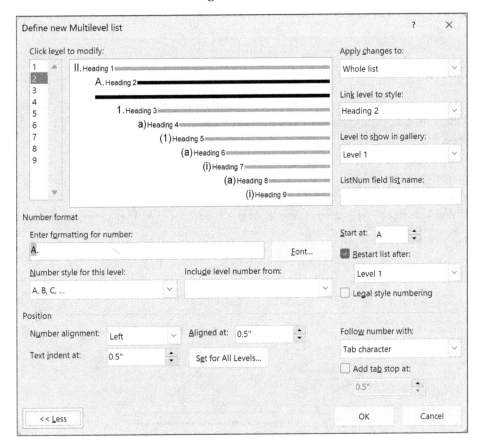

These list entries are tied into the Heading 1, Heading 2, etc. styles, which can be problematic. When I tried to add an entry using a multilevel list to the very end of an existing document that was already using Heading 1 for the chapter headers, Word automatically converted all of my prior chapter headers to parts of the multilevel list I'd just added.

You can see here that Heading 1 and Heading 2 now are formatted to be part of a multilevel list.

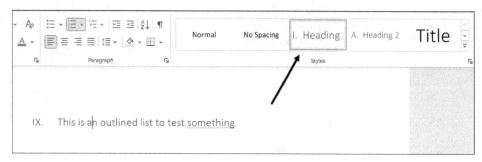

Which, hey if you're using that outline format for your entire document, is probably great, because it lets you quickly apply the multilevel list styles as needed as you write your document.

But if you were doing what I just tried to do, which is use a multilevel list at the end of the document, it's a disaster.

You can go back to that Define New Multilevel List option and change the setting that links the first level of the list to the Heading 1 style and click OK to fix that. But you need to do it for all of the levels. Here I fixed Heading 1, but you can see that Heading 2 is still tied into the multilevel list:

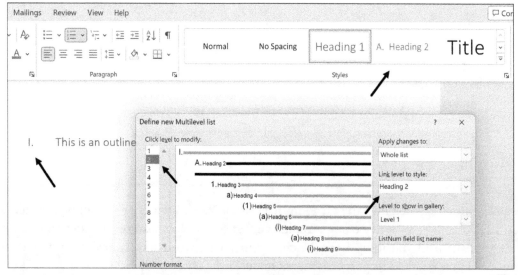

My advice to you if you want to use the multilevel list option is to make sure that your entire document uses the list and that there are no other Heading styles or other numbered or bulleted lists in the document.

Also, if you are trying to fix a document that has a multilevel list that isn't working properly, you may have to create that multilevel list in a new document and then paste in your text one paragraph at a time to fix it. (Hopefully not, but that is what I have had to do once or twice when nothing else would work.)

Not the best use of time, but it may be the only way to get it all to work the way it should.

Table of Contents

If you use styles, then you can have Word create a table of contents for you. To do that, assign Heading 1, Heading 2, etc. styles to the entries in your document that you want to include in the table of contents.

Next, go to the location in your document where you want to place the table of contents and go to the References tab. On the left-hand side is a dropdown menu for Table of Contents:

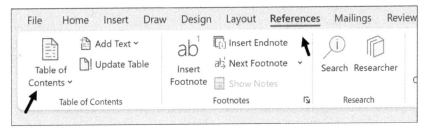

There are two pre-formatted table of content options you can choose and one manual table of contents option as well. The only difference between the two automatic tables of contents is whether it says Contents or Table of Contents. (The manual table of contents basically gives you formatting, but nothing else, so I'm not going to cover that one further.)

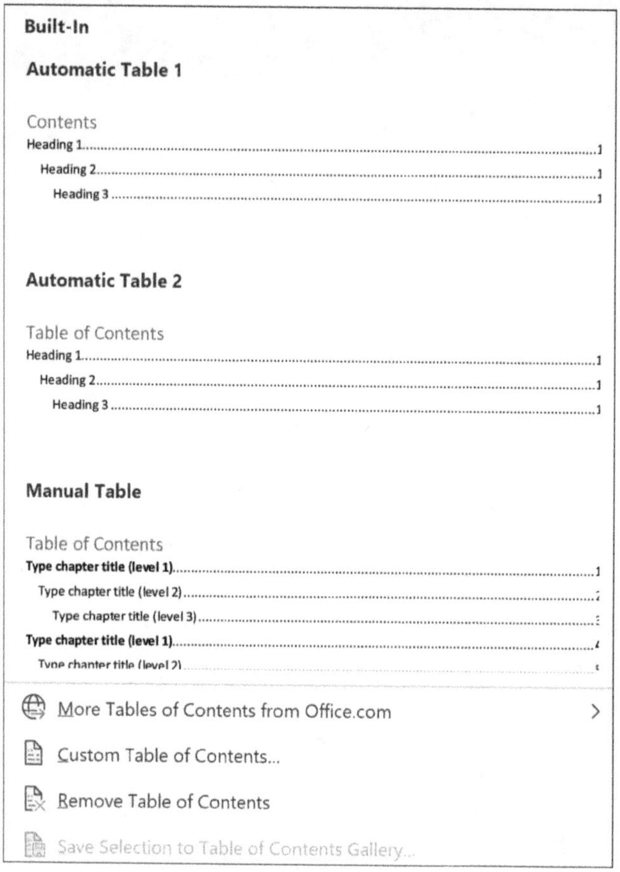

Built-In
Automatic Table 1
Contents
Heading 1.........1
Heading 2.........1
Heading 3.........1
Automatic Table 2
Table of Contents
Heading 1.........1
Heading 2.........1
Heading 3.........1
Manual Table
Table of Contents
Type chapter title (level 1).........1
Type chapter title (level 2)
Type chapter title (level 3)
Type chapter title (level 1)
More Tables of Contents from Office.com
Custom Table of Contents...
Remove Table of Contents
Save Selection to Table of Contents Gallery...

You can also use the More Tables of Contents From Office.com option or you can choose to create a Custom Table of Contents.

I'm going to choose that first option there. And here we go:

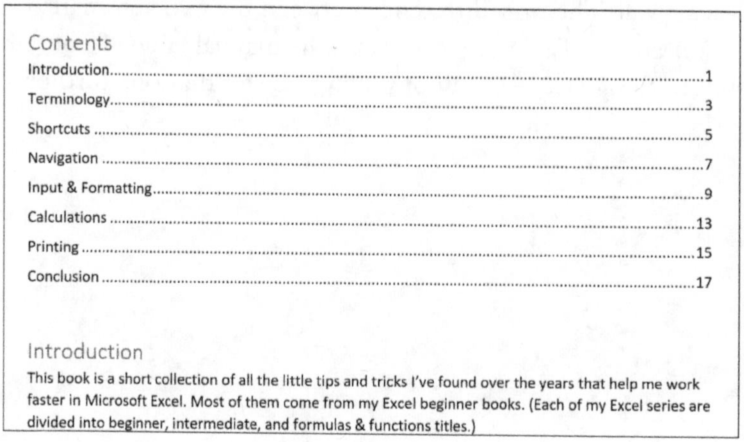

Contents
Introduction.........1
Terminology.........3
Shortcuts.........5
Navigation.........7
Input & Formatting.........9
Calculations.........13
Printing.........15
Conclusion.........17
Introduction
This book is a short collection of all the little tips and tricks I've found over the years that help me work faster in Microsoft Excel. Most of them come from my Excel beginner books. (Each of my Excel series are divided into beginner, intermediate, and formulas & functions titles.)

A few comments here. First, note that my first chapter is currently starting on the same page as my table of contents. To fix that I'd need to insert a page break. Also, I only had Heading 1 in use in this document, so I only have one level of table of contents entries for it to use.

If I go and apply Heading 2 to my sub-sections of my chapters, it doesn't automatically update. But I can right-click on the table and an Update Table option will appear at the top of the table. When I click on that I can then choose to update page numbers or the entire table in the Update Table of Contents dialogue box:

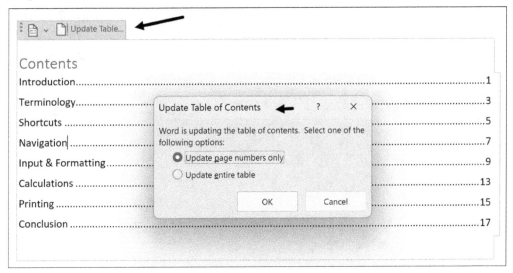

And here is my updated table of contents using Heading 1 and Heading 2:

Contents

Once you have a table of contents in your document, you can click on it and then use those three dots on the far left-hand side to left-click and drag your table of contents to a new location.

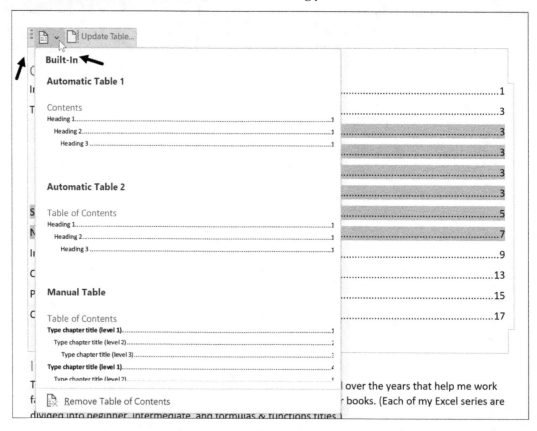

You can also click on the dropdown arrows for that little document next to the dots to bring up a dropdown menu. The bottom option in the dropdown lets you remove your table of contents.

It also displays the other default table of contents styles. You can move back and forth between Automatic Table 1 and Automatic Table 2 (just the title changes).

You can select your table of contents just like any other text in your document and change the font, but if you then update that table of contents it will revert to whatever font is being used for the entries that feed into the table.

Once there is an automatic table of contents in your document, you can use Ctrl and click on any of the entries in the table to go to that page in your document.

So what if those default styles aren't what you want? Let's go explore the Custom Table of Contents option now. Selecting that option brings up the Table of Contents dialogue box:

You can choose here whether or not to show page numbers, whether or not to right align those page numbers, what type of separator to use between the table of contents entries and the page numbers (dotted line, straight line, nothing), how many Heading levels to use to build the table of contents, and whether to use hyperlinks for the entries.

That Formats dropdown also lets you choose a variety of pre-formatted appearances that you can use for your table format.

Here for example I used a Modern Format and removed page numbers and hyperlinks:

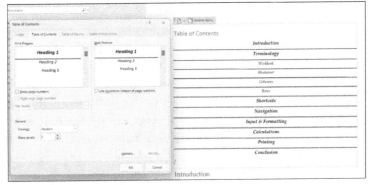

When I clicked on OK it asked if I wanted to replace my existing table of contents, so that's how to apply a new custom format to an existing table.

Unfortunately, reverting back to one of the two default automatic tables required me to delete the table of contents in my document, close it, and then re-open and insert a new table of contents. Otherwise I kept getting my custom format and would've had to manually change it back. (That could be a me issue not the program, but a workaround if you need it.)

If you want to use styles other than the Headings styles to populate your table of contents, click on Options in the Table of Contents dialogue box to bring up the Table of Contents Options dialogue box:

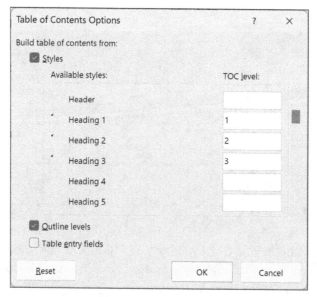

As you can see above, by default Heading 1 is the 1st level of the table of contents, Heading 2 is the 2nd level, and Heading 3 is the 3rd level, but all available styles are listed here, including any custom styles you used.

So I could remove 1 from the box for Heading 1 and put that value next to my custom style instead and then Word would use any entries with my custom style as the first level of my table of contents.

One last note, if you didn't use Headings as you created your document, you can use the Add Text option in the Table of Contents section of the References tab to assign text to the various table of content levels.

Select the text and then click on Add Text in the Table of Contents section of the References tab and choose the table of contents level you want for that text.

Word will assign that text the style that is being used for that level of your table of contents. So by default Level 1 will assign the style Heading 1. Which means you need to be careful if you don't want to change the formatting for that selected text.

Easier in my opinion to assign your styles as you work on your document, but an option if you need it.

Track Changes

Now we are up to track changes, which are amazing and wonderful and made my corporate life much, much easier.

When I first started we had a few people in my office who would manually format text to show changes. Which meant that you had to manually reformat that text to finalize the document. It was a nightmare.

With track changes, someone can make edits to your document and you can see those edits but then all you have to do is accept or reject those changes and they're incorporated into your document and you're done. It's fantastic.

Also, you can navigate through your document one change at a time so that you don't miss anything. No stray comma or period that gets skipped over because it's such a small change.

But you have to be careful with track changes. Some of the views that Word now offers with respect to track changes don't show them. So you can miss that there are track changes in a document and send it off to an outside party and they open it up and they see all of those little changes and who made them. Not a good thing.

If you use track changes, you have to be careful to accept all changes and turn them off when you're done.

Okay. Let's tackle this topic. I'm going to save comments, which go hand-in-hand with track changes, for the next chapter.

When you open a document that has track changes turned on, Word will now (as of January 2023 in Word 365) give you a warning message that track changes are on:

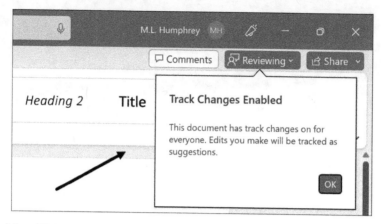

This is a good thing. You never want to work in a document that has track changes turned on without realizing you are doing so.

First things first.

Turn On or Off Track Changes

To turn on or off track changes you can use Ctrl + Shift + E. There is also an option to do so in the Tracking section of the Review tab:

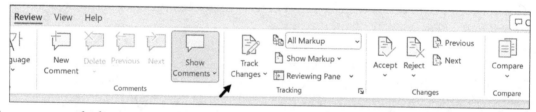

To turn on track changes, just click on that image that says Track Changes. To turn it off, click on it again. You want to click onto the image part of that option, not the text part. And you don't need the dropdown. So aim for the pen or pencil or whatever that is.

And I want to make a point here. It is possible to have a document that shows track changes, but that also has other changes that were made to the document that are not visible because someone temporarily turned off track changes and then made edits. So if it is really, really important that you see every single change in a document, use Document Compare to see all edits instead of trusting that track changes captured everything.

(Usually this is not some nefarious deliberate thing that happens. In past versions of Word I would turn off track changes when making formatting or non-essential changes to tables because the way Word showed track changes for tables was ugly and confusing and didn't really let people see what it would look like when final and most users don't want to see every little formatting change. But sometimes I'd also forget to turn it back on.)

Okay. So. Turn on track changes and make your edits.

Appearance

Here is an example of track changes with two different users:

> This is a sample document that I'm creating on my other computer to see if I can show you track changes made by two different users. It may or may not work because both of these computers are tied into the same Microsoft account. But let's give it a go.
>
> I have now turned Ttrack eChanges on in my document and you can see that any new text I add is underlined and colored a different color.
>
> This is me working on this same document on a different computer. I stripped out the Author information before I saved this version of this document so that I could appear as two different users.

Text additions that are recorded by Track Changes are underlined and color-coded. Deletions have a strikethrough and are also color-coded but are not underlined.

Above you can see that "two" in that first paragraph was deleted. And that the second and third paragraphs were all text that was added after Track Changes was turned on. The second paragraph is blue, the third is red, to indicate different users.

(For those of you reading in black and white, you won't be able to see the colors that distinguish the different users, but should still be able to see the additions and deletions.)

Also, you can see that in the second paragraph the first user wrote "track changes" and the second user changed that to "Track Changes".

For each tracked change, on the left-hand side of the text there is a vertical black line indicating that a change was made at that location.

Word automatically assigns colors to users and this can change, so you can't assume that a user will always be assigned the same color each time. The color assigned to a specific user will always be consistent within a document while that document remains open, but the color assigned to a user can change when the document is reopened

For example, when I wrote that first paragraph on my old laptop the changes were in red. But when I opened that document on my new laptop the changes were in blue. So you need to check each time when you review a document which user is assigned to which color.

Users

All changes made when Track Changes are turned on are assigned to users. By default, each user is assigned their own color. This is normally based upon the associated Microsoft Office account of the user, not the computer.

So, for example, when I worked on a document on one computer and then transferred it to another, my changes on the new computer were given the same color because both computers are tied into my Microsoft Office account. (I was able to get the two colors you can see in the example above only when I stripped the author information from the document after I made the first set of edits.)

To see who the user is for a specific edit, you have a couple options.

The first option is to hold your mouse over the edit:

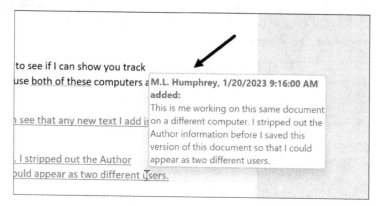

Note that also shows the time and date when the edit was made.

The second option is to show the Reviewing Pane.

Reviewing Pane

The Reviewing Pane can be turned on or off using the Reviewing Pane dropdown menu in the Tracking section of the Review tab:

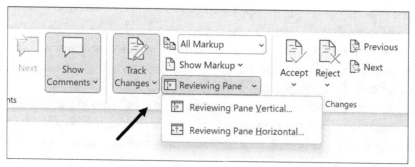

You have the choice of a vertical pane or a horizontal pane. My preference is for the vertical pane, although usually I don't actually use a reviewing pane at all:

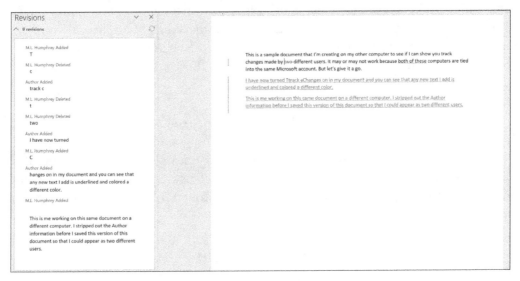

The Reviewing Pane will list each revision in the document as well as who made that revision. So you can see here that the two users that Word is tracking are Author and M.L. Humphrey.

The reason I'm not a huge fan of using it for simple track changes is because it's much easier for me to see what's happening in the document itself than to interpret that list of revisions.

For example, here:

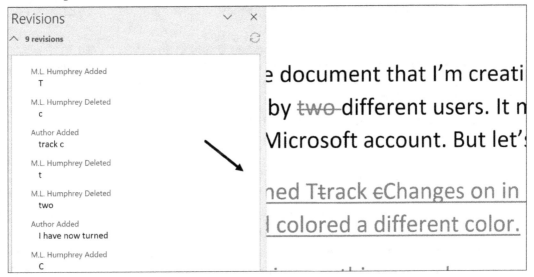

It's pretty easy looking at the text to see that one user wrote the words "track changes" and that another user came along and capitalized them so that it became "Track Changes".

But if I look in the Revisions panel, I have listings that tell me M.L. Humphrey added "T" and deleted "c" and that Author added "track c" and that M.L. Humphrey deleted "t" and then it lists two unrelated edits and finally tells me that M.L. Humphrey added "C".

The list of revisions is accurate, but reading through those edits one at a time is confusing. So I don't do it usually.

Track Changes Views

I personally like this view that's the default view for my track changes, All Markup. It shows me the old text as well as all edits that have been made. This is the view I try to keep active at all times unless I need a different view. But let's walk through those other choices in case you need them.

Simple Markup

This is the Simple Markup view:

This is a sample document that I'm creating on my other computer to see if I can show you track changes made by different users. It may or may not work because both of these computers are tied into the same Microsoft account. But let's give it a go.

I have now turned Track Changes on in my document and you can see that any new text I add is underlined and colored a different color.

This is me working on this same document on a different computer. I stripped out the Author information before I saved this version of this document so that I could appear as two different users.

It has a red vertical line off to the side to indicate where edits have been made, but, other than that, it's the final document with all changes made.

It's good for seeing what the final product will look like. So a good last-pass option. It makes sure that you catch any extra spaces or double periods or things like that that can slip through when track changes are on.

But for me it is not a good working option. Many times I found as I was working with teams on projects that I really did need to know what was originally written, how that was changed, and who made the change. Hate to say it, but if the lawyer with twenty years of experience made the edit to that technical paragraph that was written by the brand new analyst I'm more likely to trust that edit was correct than if the brand new analyst edited something written by the lawyer. Context often matters.

No Markup

This is the No Markup view:

> This is a sample document that I'm creating on my other computer to see if I can show you track changes made by different users. It may or may not work because both of these computers are tied into the same Microsoft account. But let's give it a go.
>
> I have now turned Track Changes on in my document and you can see that any new text I add is underlined and colored a different color.
>
> This is me working on this same document on a different computer. I stripped out the Author information before I saved this version of this document so that I could appear as two different users.

It has no indication that there are any track changes in the document. The text reflects all of the changes that were made. But there is no way to see that track changes is on.

I would use this one only if I were printing off a copy of the document for review by a senior person who needed to review the "final" but where I wasn't yet willing to remove tracked changes yet. It would allow printing of a completely clean copy and wouldn't distract that senior person with notations of where changes had been made.

But I'd immediately get away from this view as soon as I printed the document. I would never leave a document in this view.

(As someone whose job used to be investigating financial institutions for rule violations that sometimes carried hefty fines, trust me that you don't want to forget that a document has track changes still visible.)

Original

This is the Original view:

> This is a sample document that I'm creating on my other computer to see if I can show you track changes made by two different users. It may or may not work because both of these computers are tied into the same Microsoft account. But let's give it a go.

This is another one I would never, ever leave my document in for any length of time. But sometimes it can be helpful to look at the document as it existed prior to any edits. Especially when there are multiple users making edits to the same text. That lets you see what the source text really was.

All Markup

And then finally, as a reminder, this is the All Markup view:

> This is a sample document that I'm creating on my other computer to see if I can show you track changes made by ~~two~~ different users. It may or may not work because both of these computers are tied into the same Microsoft account. But let's give it a go.
>
> I have now turned Ttrack eChanges on in my document and you can see that any new text I add is underlined and colored a different color.
>
> This is me working on this same document on a different computer. I stripped out the Author information before I saved this version of this document so that I could appear as two different users.

It shows the original text in black and then marks the location of any changes with a black vertical line off to the side of the text. All additions and deletions in the document are shown with colored text. For me, this is the best one to see what was done to the original text and whether I agree.

A Quick Warning

If it matters to you who made what changes in your document, then never ever do what I did above to give you these examples. I achieved that effect by stripping out the Author information from the document. And right now that All Markup example looks great. It has changes by two distinct users and we can see what each of them did. But as soon as I save changes to that document, all of the changes will be assigned to Author.

I had this happen on a big project. Some analyst stripped out the author information from the original document and then circulated it to a team of six for edits. And no one noticed what was happening until we had a final document where all edits appeared as if they'd been made by one user. It was horrible.

So if you must strip out the author information from a document, save a copy of that document as it existed right before you do that and then strip those properties out of your document only when the document is final and ready to be distributed. Never strip author information from a document that is still a work in progress that may require the use of track changes.

Show Markup Options

One final basic appearance setting that we have not yet covered is the Show Markup dropdown menu available in the Tracking section of the Review tab:

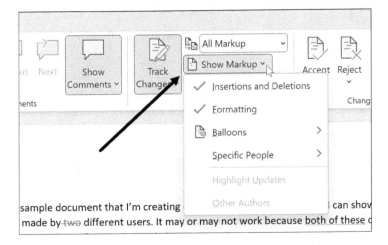

By default, Word will show both insertions/deletions and formatting changes. Here is an example with formatting changes included:

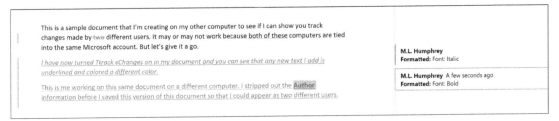

There are times when you really don't need to see all the formatting changes. I am a control freak so I always wanted to see them, but for a lawyer whose focus is on the words and the commas, they don't need to see that you reformatted the headers throughout the document.

So if you don't want to see the formatting changes listed out, click on that option to turn it off. Or if you do want to see them and they're off, click on that option to turn it on.

You can also choose how changes in the document are shown. By default, only formatting changes are shown in "balloons" which are the notes off to the side, but you can actually choose to show all revisions that way or to show all revisions inline in the document:

Here is an example that shows revisions in balloons:

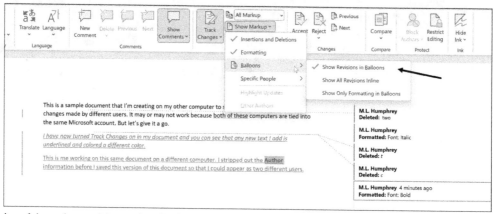

The nice thing about this setting is that it takes out deleted text from your document so you still can see changes in the document but you don't have to mentally remove the deleted text. See the Track Changes example there in the second paragraph as an example of how that works.

Show revisions inline basically is what you saw above with the All Markup screenshot, but this time there's no note off to the side to call-out the formatting changes. They're just there with no specific mention that they were made. (So not a setting I personally like to use.)

Finally, you can choose to only see edits from specific people if you want. Again, personally, not something I would do because I was always looking at the entirety of the document and whether the entire thing worked as a final report. But I'm sure there are times when it makes sense to hide the edits made by one specific user. For example, maybe if an analyst reformatted the document with track changes on and you don't want those changes flagged during your review.

Advanced Options

You can customize track changes by clicking on the expansion arrow in the Tracking section of the Review tab to open the Track Changes Options dialogue box:

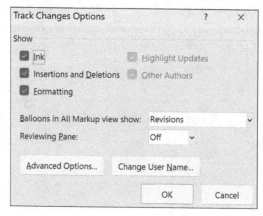

That allows you to then click on Advanced Options to open the Advanced Track Changes Options dialogue box:

Advanced Track Changes Options	?	×
Markup		

Insertions: Underline   Color: By author

Deletions: Strikethrough   Color: By author

Changed lines: Outside border

Moves

☐ Track moves

Moved from: Double strikethrough   Color: Green

Moved to: Double underline   Color: Green

Table cell highlighting

Inserted cells: Light Blue   Merged cells: Light Yellow

Deleted cells: Pink   Split cells: Light Orange

Formatting

☑ Track formatting

Formatting: (none)   Color: By author

Balloons

Preferred width: 3.7"   Measure in: Inches

Margin: Right

☑ Show lines connecting to text

Paper orientation in printing: Preserve

OK   Cancel

This is where you can change the colors used for tracking changes as well as how tracked changes are shown in the document. So you could set it so that there is just one color used for all changes regardless of the author and you could even choose what that color is.

I want to say back in the day legal documents used a double black-line strikethrough for deletions, for example. This is where you could set your document to do that.

Just know that this is a personal setting that will apply for your version of the document, but not for someone else looking at the same document.

Okay, now that we've covered all of the appearance settings, time to actually review the changes and accept them or reject them.

Review Changes

To review the changes in your document, you can turn on the Reviewing Pane and scroll through that way, but what I prefer is to either read the document or, if there are scattered or small changes, use the Previous and Next options in the Changes section of the Review tab:

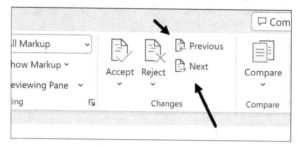

Click on Next to move forward to the next change in the document. Word will move through the document, find the next change, and highlight it. Click on Previous to move backward through the document.

Accept or Reject Changes

In that same section, you have the option to Accept or Reject. Both of those have a dropdown menu with a variety of choices.

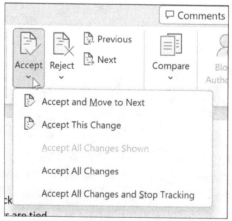

Here you can see that for Accept the options are to accept and move to next, accept this change, accept all changes, or accept all changes and stop tracking.

I tend not to accept or reject a single change at a time. And the reason for that is what you can see with that track changes edit. Word considers that six separate changes. First was the addition of track and changes, then was the deletion of the lower-case t and c, and then was the addition of the upper-case t and c.

Rather than walk through those six changes and accept them individually, what I do is select both words and then click on Accept. That accepts all six changes at once.

So usually I walk through a document using previous and next, read that phrase, sentence, or paragraph, make any additional edits I think are needed and then select the whole thing and accept the edits. (Assuming this is a final pass that no one else needs to review. Obviously, don't accept all changes if someone needs to see what you did.)

Turn Off Track Changes

When you are done with your document and all changes have been made and accepted, turn off track changes. Yes, I have said this ten times. I probably need to say it ten more. DO NOT leave track changes turned on in your document. One, it's a nuisance if you then go to make any edit whatsoever to the document. And, two, you do not want to run the risk of circulating a "final" document that actually has a bunch of tracked changes in it.

When track changes is on, your status in the top right corner will be Reviewing and when it is off your status will be Editing.

Final Document Review

Before you finalize your document, you can have Word review the document for any lingering tracked changes that weren't accepted or rejected.

To do so, go to the File tab and then click on Info. There is an option there to Inspect Document. Click on Check for Issues to see if there are still tracked changes present in the document:

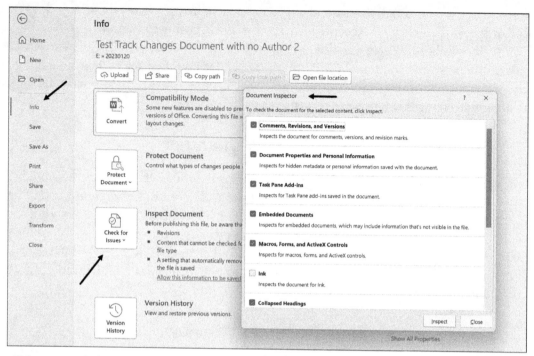

It will be part of the Comments, Revisions, and Versions option.

(Just be careful about removing your document properties and personal information, which I warned about above. That is under Document Properties and Personal Information.)

Comments

For me, comments in Word go hand-in-hand with track changes, but they're actually two separate things, so I've separated them into two separate chapters. Here is an example of a comment and the beginning of a response:

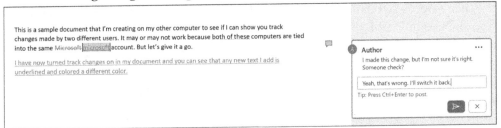

You can see that by default comments are visible off to the side of the main text and that the document will have a little comment bubble there to the right of the text to indicate the existence of a comment.

I left the response unfinished so you could also see that tip that says to use Ctrl + Enter to post a response. If you just use Enter, it goes to a new line within the comment. Your other option for finalizing a comment is to click on that blue button with the arrow in it.

Here is what it looks like when someone has made a comment and then someone else has responded to that comment:

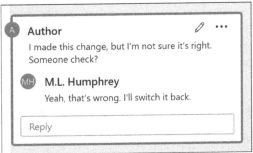

To edit a response, just hold your cursor over it and you'll see the pencil appear next to the name of the person who commented. Click on that and then make your changes.

One fault in Word is that you can actually edit someone else's comment. So I can click on that little pencil in the top right corner of the comment box and edit the comment made by Author even though I'm currently M.L. Humphrey to Word.

Alright. So how do you add a comment in the first place?

Place your cursor at the location in the document where you want to make a comment and then go to the Comments section of the Review tab and click on New Comment:

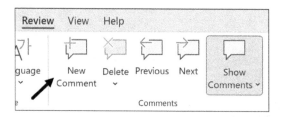

You can also use Ctrl + Alt + M or right-click and choose New Comment from the dropdown menu. When you click on that option, Word will insert a new comment window with the cursor in the beginning of the comment window. You can either type your text and then use Ctrl + Enter or the button with the blue arrow to add that comment or click on the X if you changed your mind.

While a comment is selected, Word shifts it to the left like you can see below with the middle comment.

When no comments are selected they all align.

The Delete option in the Comments section will let you delete the current comment, delete all comments in the document, or delete all resolved comments. You can also click on an individual comment and then right-click on the ... in the top right corner and choose Delete Thread to delete a comment and any responses.

To Resolve a comment, right-click on the ... in the top right corner of the comment and then choose to Resolve Thread:

The comment will be marked as Resolved and grayed out, but will still appear in your document:

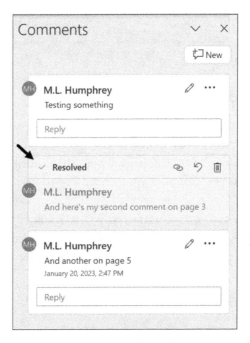

This option is not available if you are in Compatibility Mode, so have opened a .doc file instead of a .docx file.

The Show Comments dropdown in the Comments section has two options, Contextual or List. Contextual places the comments next to where they were made in the document. List shows all comments from the document in a Comments task pane:

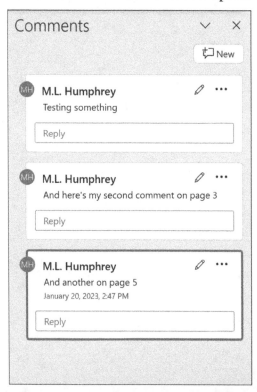

The comments are all listed together regardless of what page they appear on. Above, for example, there were comments I made on page 1, page 3, and page 5. Even when I scroll to page 7, all three of those comments are listed in that task pane. Whereas with the Contextual option they only show when you're on the page where the comment was made.

If you are in the List view, you can click on a comment to go to the page that contains that comment.

You can make comments on a document even when Track Changes are turned off.

If you have track changes in a document that display in a balloon off to the right side, any comments will be pushed to the right of those tracked changes and may not be readily visible.

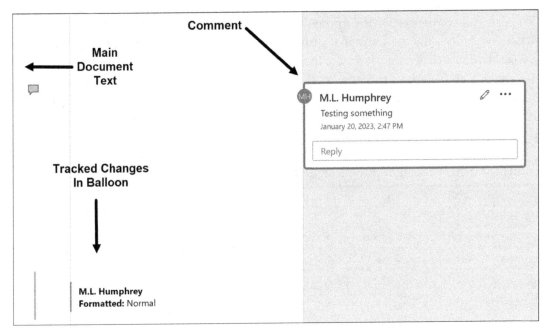

You can fix this by setting tracked changes to display inline.

Another option is to click on the Comments button in the top right corner of the workspace to open the Comments task pane to see the text of your comments, but that task pane will appear on top of any tracked changes balloons. If you close the Navigation task pane, however, then you can have the Comments task pane visible as well as any tracked changes shown in balloons.

You can use the Previous and Next options in the Comments section of the Review tab to move through the comments in your document.

However, Word will skip any comments that have been marked as resolved. Furthermore, it will not show those comments off to the side with your active comments. They will only be indicated by the comment icon to the right of your text.

Here is one open comment with the comment displayed and then you can see the comment bubble for a resolve comment below that:

You can still see the resolved comment by clicking on that comment bubble.

Also, you cannot make a comment directly on a footnote or endnote. (That would be very nice to have Microsoft people, if you're looking for things you can do to improve the program.)

If you're used to how comments worked previously in Word, including with a dotted line between the comment and text it was addressing, you can currently revert back to the old way of doing things by going to the File tab and then Options and the General page and unchecking the box for Enable Modern Comments.

Here's how that used to look with a dotted line between the comment and where in the document someone was trying to place that comment:

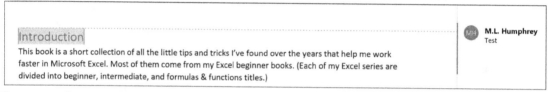

They are going to retire the ability to switch back at some point, but for now it's still an option. You may have to close Word and reopen before that change takes effect, though.

Compare Documents

The final aspect to track changes and comments is comparing documents. I mentioned it before, because it's the most sure-fire way to know that you're seeing all changes that were made to a document. You take the original document, you take the new document, and you give them both to Word and tell it to flag any changes.

But it can also be a bit messy at times especially if text was moved around. Still, it's nice to know about if you need it.

First step, open a new document in Word. Go to the Review tab and find the Compare dropdown in the Compare section on the right-hand side. Click on Compare.

The Compare Documents dialogue box will appear:

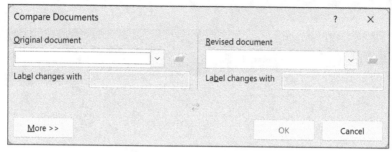

The left-hand side is the original of the document. The right-hand side is the updated version. Click on the dropdown menu to see recent documents you've used and select one of those files or use the little folder to the right of the dropdown to go find your file.

Word will automatically populate the Label Changes With field with a user name, but you can change that if you want.

Click on More to tell Word which changes to identify and how to treat changes like the one we talked about before with "track changes" being changed to "Track Changes".

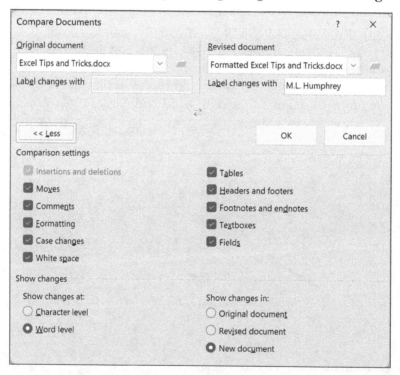

If you choose to show changes at the character level then it will look like the example from above. If you choose to show at the word level it will show that as a deletion of track changes replaced with an insertion of Track Changes instead of just changes to the individual letters.

You can also choose whether to show those changes in the original document, the revised document, or a new document. The default is new document which is what I always choose as well.

Click on OK when you're done. Here we go:

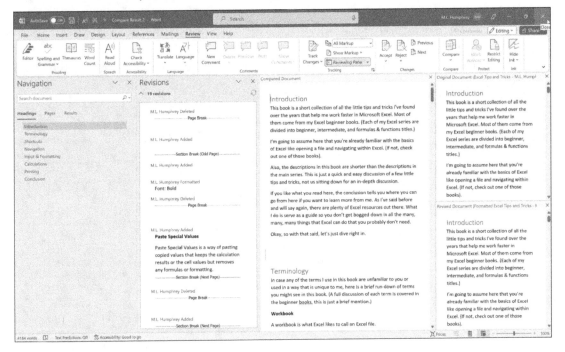

That looks chaotic, but we can hide the Navigation pane and that leaves me with a Revisions pane on the left-hand side, the new document in the center and then the original document on the top right and the revised document on the bottom right.

Click on an edit in the Revisions pane to go to that section of the other documents:

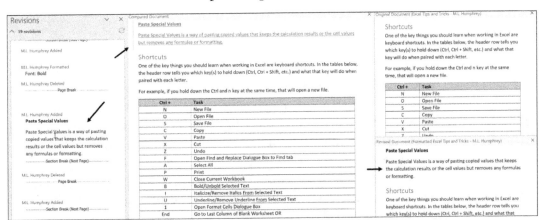

You can see above, for example, a change I made where I added text related to Paste Special Values within the document. Word recorded that as adding text. You can see it reflected as a tracked change in the new document, see that that text was not in the original, and see that text in the revised document.

I often find with document compare that I just want to view the new comparison document. You can do that by clicking on the X in the corner of the original and revised documents to close them.

That also makes the page breaks in the new comparison document appear, which helps me understand what this particular change was:

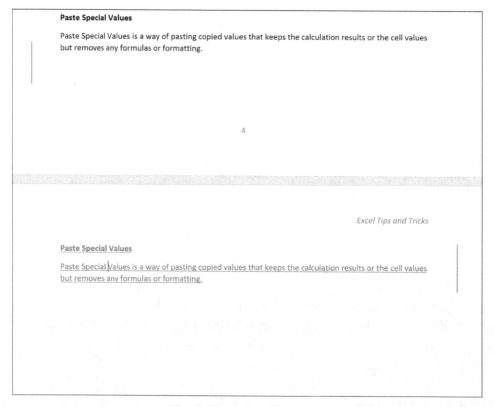

Now I can see (and remember) that what I did here was copy text from the end of that chapter and paste it in there so that I would force the chapter start to the next page. I did that so I could demonstrate a specific type of section break. The fact that the text was not part of the next chapter was not obvious if you look at the screenshot above this one because Word in that view was not showing page and section breaks on the screen.

But you can see that what I ended up with was a document that has track changes that reflect formatting changes, the addition/deletion of page and section breaks, and the addition of headers and footers as well.

Usually I only need this when a document was edited but not in track changes. I have also used it when someone edited a document and some of the changes I made to their edits were to reject additions or deletions they made, which you can't see in track changes at the end.

So what I did in that situation is accepted all changes in their version and then compared that document to my final version after I had accepted or rejected their changes. That left me with a document where the only track changes in the document were edits on their edits.

Okay. We're getting towards the end, but let's quickly cover footnotes and endnotes and then maybe a few tiny items.

Chapter Eight

Footnotes and Endnotes

Footnotes and Endnotes can both be added to a document from the Footnotes section of the References tab. The main option there is to Insert Footnote but there is also an option to Insert Endnote.

Click at the point you want to insert your note and then click on the option you want to use. Word will automatically insert the note on that page (for a footnote) or at the end of the document (for an endnote). The note will be below a line and will have a superscript number both at the point of insertion and in that footnote or endnote section:

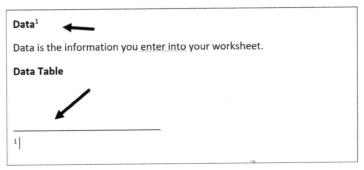

Type whatever text you want to type for the note and then click back into the main document.

You can see the text of a note you've added to your document at that point in the document by holding your mouse over the number:

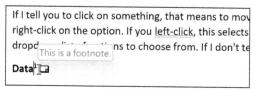

Here I have my mouse over the 1 next to Data and I can see the text "This is a footnote" that I added as my footnote.

To delete a footnote or endnote, just delete that number from within your text.

If you want to convert a footnote to an endnote or vice versa, right-click on the note and choose the Convert to [X] option from the dropdown menu.

There is also a Note Options choice in the dropdown menu. Click on that to open the Footnote and Endnote dialogue box:

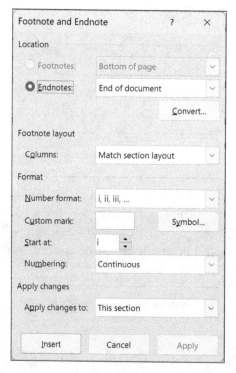

This allows you to choose the numbering style and formatting of the notes in your document.

If you need to navigate between the footnotes or endnotes in your document, the Footnotes section of the References tab has a dropdown under Next Footnote that allows you to either go to the next footnote, previous footnote, next endnote, or previous endnote in the document.

Miscellaneous Topics

Real quick I'm going to mention a few topics we're not covering in detail here.

Insert Citations, Captions, or Index Entries

The References tab also has options for inserting citations, captions, index entries, or a table of authorities.

Dictation

Word does have a dictation option in the Voice section of the Home tab.

Hyperlink

If you need to provide a website link, you can use the Link option in the Links section of the Insert tab. This also lets you link to other documents, other locations within the document, or to an email address.

Word Themes

If you don't like the default Word theme, there are a number of additional choices on the Design tab.

Line Numbering

You can add line numbering from the Page Setup section of the Layout tab.

Hyphenation

You can hyphenate the text in your paragraphs from the Page Setup section of the Layout tab.

Mail Merge

You can create mail merge documents using the Mailings tab. This usually requires integration with an Excel spreadsheet that has your list of recipients and their related information.

Read Aloud

You can have Word read your document aloud to you using the Read Aloud option in the Speech section of the Review tab. Note that the voice it uses if you are offline is much less natural sounding than the one it uses if you are online, at least by default.

Online Collaboration

It is possible to have multiple people editing the same document at the same time using online collaboration tools in Word. (I personally think that's a nightmare scenario, but I do know author teams who use it.)

Sort

If you ever have a list of entries that you need to sort alphabetically, you can do so using the Sort option in the Paragraph section of the Home tab which shows an A on top of a Z with a downpointing arrow.

You can use this with tables but I also have used it in the past with a list of text entries that I wanted to alphabetize quickly. As long as they're on separate lines, they're easy to sort.

Conclusion

Alright. That was *Intermediate Word 365*. It was not everything you can do in Word. As you can see from that last chapter, there are a good dozen topics right there that I could have covered in another forty pages or so that I chose to only mention. And there are other things you can do in Word that I didn't mention at all, like everything covered in the Draw tab.

The service I provide with these books is giving you a path through the wide variety of things you can do in Word so that you don't get lost while trying to learn what you need to learn. But it is entirely possible that I did not cover something you need to know, like mail merges.

The first step when there's something you want to learn about in Word is to, if you know where it is already, hold your mouse over that option:

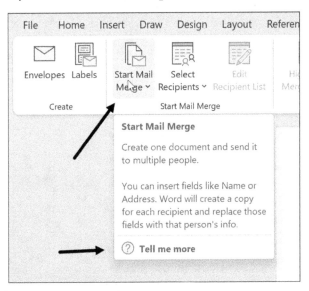

Often there will be a Tell Me More link at the bottom of the basic description that Word gives for that task. Click on that option and Word's help task pane will open to a help topic specific to that task.

If that isn't available, you can go to the Help tab and click on one of the help options there. F1 will also open the Help task pane. You have to be online to use Word's help these days but it is very helpful.

Another option if that doesn't work is a web search for your topic combined with the words "Word 365" or "Microsoft Office Word" and then whatever it is you're trying to learn about.

Microsoft's help is generally very good for how something works. They're less helpful when it comes to "is this possible" type questions. But the internet is vast and somewhere out there it is very likely that someone has already provided the answer to your question if you just look for it. Sometimes knowing what to search for is a bit tricky if you don't know the terms, but 9 times out of 10 or more like 999 out of 1000 the answer is out there.

For example, when I was writing this book and my columns weren't evening out I thought, "that should be possible, shouldn't it?" so I did an internet search and found a website that had told how to do it back in 2006. Perfect.

And if you ever have confusion about anything I covered here or just want to ask me about something, reach out. I'm happy to help. I can't guarantee an immediate response, but I usually will see an email and respond within a few days.

Okay, then. Good luck with it. Don't be afraid to experiment. Ctrl + Z, Undo, is your friend. And remember that sometimes if a document with really complex formatting starts doing strange things to you, the best bet is to strip all of that formatting out and start over, as painful as that thought might be.

Index

113

About the Author

M.L. Humphrey is a former stockbroker with a degree in Economics from Stanford and an MBA from Wharton who has spent close to twenty years as a regulator and consultant in the financial services industry.

You can reach M.L. at mlhumphreywriter@gmail.com or at mlhumphrey.com.